THE BEST AMERICAN NEWSPAPER NARRATIVES OF 2012

THE BEST AMERICAN NEWSPAPER NARRATIVES OF 2012

George Getschow, editor

Writer-in-Residence, The Mayborn
Literary Nonfiction Conference

Number 1 in the Mayborn Best
American Newspaper Narrative Series

University of North Texas Press

Mayborn Graduate Institute of Journalism

Denton, Texas

10 9 8 7 6 5 4 3 2 1

Permissions:
University of North Texas Press
1155 Union Circle #311336
Denton, TX 76203-5017

The paper used in this book meets the minimum requirements of the
American National Standard for Permanence of Paper for Printed Library
Materials, z39.48.1984. Binding materials have been chosen for durability.

Library of Congress Cataloging-in-Publication Data

The best American newspaper narratives of 2012 /
edited by George Getschow, writer-in-residence,
The Mayborn Literary Nonfiction Conference.

pages cm. -- (Number 1 in the Mayborn
best American newspaper narrative series)

ISBN 978-1-57441-549-0 (pbk. : alk. paper) --

1. Journalism--Awards--United States. 2. Feature stories—United
States. 3. Reportage literature, American. 4. People with social
disabilities--United States. 5. People with social disabilities—
Press coverage--United States. I. Getschow, George, 1950- editor
II. Saslow, Eli. Life of a salesman. III. Mayborn Literary Nonfiction
Conference. IV. Mayborn Graduate Institute of Journalism. V.
Series: Mayborn best American newspaper narrative series ; no. 1.

PN4726.B37 2014

071'.3079--dc23

2014006266

The Best American Newspaper Narratives of 2012 is Number
1 in the Mayborn Best American Newspaper Narrative Series

The electronic edition of this book was made possible
by the support of the Vick Family Foundation.

TABLE OF CONTENTS

LIST OF FIGURES

The Best American Newspaper Narratives of 2012

The Best American Newspaper Narratives of 2012

George Getschow

In American literature, whether fiction or nonfiction, the best narratives capture the absurdities, the contradictions, the paradoxes, the sadnesses and the glories of everyday life in the poetry of everyday speech. The best American narratives arouse powerful feelings from deep inside us. When they fail, no matter how well-crafted the story, no matter how important the subject—readers stop reading because they *expect* to feel something.

That's why the best American narratives require deep thinking and sound planning. They can't be reported or written in haste, on a tight deadline, with a snarky editor breathing down your neck. "Where's the story Myrtle? Don't you know we have a paper to put out?"

Unlike most news and feature stories that appear in the daily editions of newspapers across America, stories that stick to a tried-and-true form, if not a formula, narratives are in many ways formless. Young writers often ask me if there's some kind of master plan, some method, for both discovering and constructing a great narrative. I tell them no. Narratives come in all forms, shapes and sizes. There are event-driven narratives, place-driven narratives, time-driven narratives, memory-driven narratives and many others. There's no one model, one true form, that fits real world experiences.

The only certainty, I tell young writers, is that in the end, their stories will almost never turn out as expected. Finding, shaping and forming a great narrative is always a great mystery. You have to fumble around in the dark, praying you'll somehow stumble across a sympathetic character who arouses your curiosity, someone driven by a need, an obsession, a quest, a lofty ambition that's likely to present them with mighty difficulties, but also the allure of achievement.

Once you find her—say a beautiful young woman who wants to become a man—you know she is going to face a world of misery to achieve her ambition. You want to follow her journey, to see if she succeeds or fails. You're not sure, exactly, what her story is all about, not yet anyway. Why is she doing this? How much pain and embarrassment can she tolerate going through the process? And if her transformation is successful, will *he* be accepted on the other side of the gender divide? Will *he* find happiness?

As the days, weeks and months pass, your editor is growing increasingly nervous. You assure him you now know what the story is about; you're just waiting for "the resolution," some neat and tidy ending to the story. But as more weeks pass you realize that there is no neat and tidy ending, no "resolution" of your character's problems, no solid answers to the questions you really wanted to know.

Like life itself, because narratives mirror reality. The best endings, I tell young writers, leave the reader thinking about your character: What will happen to her? Will she ever escape her troubles? Will the character who is now a he ever realize his quest, the thing he said he wanted more than anything in the world? Only Hollywood, I tell them, produces neat and tidy endings.

***

Yet while there's no exact formula or form for telling great nonfiction narratives, there are things they all have in common. The best nonfiction narratives have a distinct attitude, an unmistakable tone, like the clink of a wine glass. That tone might be harsh, humorous, sarcastic, sweet, bitter or a combination of these. A narrative exploring a married woman's unrequited need for romance, for example, might well start out with a humorous tone before the woman succumbs to temptation and tragedy takes over, laying hold of her, her husband, and her lover.

The best nonfiction narratives have a clear time line, a chronology in which the story unfolds, tension and conflict arises, causing trouble for a character but pleasure for readers, who can only wonder, "What will happen next?" The chronology is usually linear, but sometimes the writer will deliberately play with chronology to create suspense or some other dramatic effect. But the best nonfiction narratives never alter reality in a way that makes the story untruthful or unreliable.

The best nonfiction narratives transform place and landscape into a gritty, deeply felt force that shapes and defines the characters. Landscape and place are often inextricably bound up with the characters—in their memories, feelings and experiences. A place, a landscape, a setting is often the epicenter of personal significance and psychological identity, shaping people's perceptions and interpretations of reality. In the best nonfiction narratives, place and landscape are transformed into living, breathing entities, facing the same tensions and conflicts as their characters.

The best nonfiction narratives have something vital at stake—freedom, failure, equality, stability, mobility, identity, destruction, preservation, temptation, you name it—forcing the characters to make choices that set them off on perilous journeys or quests with no end in sight, at least no end the reader can envision.

The best nonfiction narratives have an emotional goal—to move people and effect change. That can only happen when the story connects with the deepest core of a reader's psychological and spiritual being. The connection must be strong and deeply felt, forming an emotional bond between the writer, the reader, and the subject. Making that connection may be the hardest part of the narrative craft.

Finally, the best nonfiction narratives reveal something beyond the story itself, some universal truth, some profound insight or understanding that sheds new light on the living and the dead. "Big truths," says Gene Weingarten, an acclaimed narrative writer for the *Washington Post*, "usually contain somewhere within them the specter of death. Death informs virtually all of literature. We lust and love so we can feel more alive. We build families so we can be immortal. We crave fame, and do good works, so both will outlive us. The gods of our choosing promise eternity."

***

In selecting *The Best American Newspaper Narratives of 2012*, I know our jurists took into account the literary value of each submission, weighing, for example, everything from the writer's choice of language, attention to detail, use of scenes, settings, characterization, point of view, dialogue—all the literary devices that make it possible for the reader to see and hear and feel, as if first hand, the actual experience.

But did they consider Gene Weingarten's measure of the literary in weighing the stories submitted to them? Did they pause and ponder whether these narratives contained, somewhere within them, the specter of death? I don't know. What I do know is that in different ways, the ten *Best American Newspaper Narratives* in this collection do grapple with deaths: the death of the American dream; the death of opportunity for a teenager stuck in the Rust Belt; the death of a Wisconsin family's notions of gender and identity; the death of fear and embarrassment in two teenagers living in a homeless shelter; the slow, lingering death of racism exposed through the hard fall of a favorite son in a small Ohio town. Death comes to a teenager's loyalty to a murderous gang in Norfolk, VA; to an "iteration of blackness" that didn't fully express the truths and complexities of a bi-racial poet; to an American soldier's enmity toward Afghans suffering through a never-ending war; and to a smug sense of invincibility the day a mountain moves.

Fortunately, there's much more than the specter of death hovering over *The Best American Newspaper Narratives of 2012*. These are stories that do what the acclaimed essayist Scott Russell Sanders says all great stories do: They entertain us, create community and kinship. They help us to see through the eyes of other people. They show us the consequence of our own actions. They educate our desires, help us dwell in place, help us deal with suffering, loss and death, teach us how to be human, acknowledge the wonders and mysteries of Creation.

Eli Saslow's "Life of a Salesman" explores the anxiety and doubt surrounding a once highly successful pool salesman getting pummeled by the recession. Saslow skillfully transforms the salesman's car into a shelter from the economic storm buffeting his optimism and sense of self-worth. "He loved being in the car," Saslow writes, "the one place that was his alone, where he could fortify himself against stress and negativity. There was Motrin in the center console for his headaches, hand sanitizer for germs and four empty bags of pistachios, because cracking shells occupied his hands and quieted his mind. There was classic rock on the radio, because he had changed the station when the host of his favorite conservative talk show started dissecting the economy, a word Frank couldn't stand to say or hear, because he had come to equate it with 'an excuse for failure,' he said. There was a Bible open in the back seat, because having it there occasionally helped seal the deal with a religious customer, but mostly because Frank was an ardent believer who liked to read and annotate the book when his faith needed restoration."

Saslow earned first place in the Mayborn's Best American Newspaper Narrative Writing Contest and was a finalist for the Pulitzer Prize in feature writing.

Kelley Benham's "Never Let Go" sounds the deepest meaning of motherhood and the healing power of love. Her baby was born at 23 weeks, which her doctors considered the very edge of viability and leaving them less than optimistic about her chances of survival. "I clenched and vomited as he (the obstetrician) explained that our baby had no chance outside the womb, if she wasn't already gone."

But Juniper did survive. And the following summer, Benham decided to return to the hospital to interview all the people "who took care of her about the scientific and ethical challenges of trying to save babies born so soon." As she interviewed all the people who had saved her daughter's life, Kelley had to teach herself to separate her emotions from her journalism or, as she put it, "to step in-and-out of character."

What was conceived as a hybrid personal essay and reported narrative now posed the biggest challenge of Benham's career, and she knew her high ambition for the story was no slam dunk. "If this isn't the best thing I've ever written," she told her editor, "don't put it in the paper."

He did put it in the paper, and it not only was selected second place in the Mayborn's Best American Newspaper Narrative Writing Contest, it was also selected as a finalist by the Pulitzer Prize Committee.

Anne Hull's "Breaking Free," set in New Castle, PA, the heart of the Rust Belt, is an astonishingly well-rendered evocation of a shabby place growing shabbier each year. The writer takes a deep-dive into the substrata of New Castle society, exploring the vanishing opportunities of the town's youth who not long ago belonged to America's prosperous, upwardly mobile middle class.

Retail and food service jobs outnumbered manufacturing jobs in the country. A church fundraising drive for kids has turned into fast cash for parents who decided to hawk donated Auntie Anne's pretzels for themselves. As students became poorer, SAT scores dropped precipitously. And trips to cash in $20-off coupons at the outlet mall became the only kind of "shopping" students could afford. Signs were everywhere in New Castle that "the promise of the middle class ... had moved farther from their reach," Hull writes.

Which explains why 17-year-old Tabitha Rouzzo, who lived in a rent house two blocks from the projects, kept her mind on the college catalogues arriving in her mailbox "like gift-wrapped presents against white aluminum siding gone dingy from decades of wear." The ambitious teenager was counting on college to escape "her mother's destiny" in New Castle. But when her SAT results came in well below the national average, Tabitha had to settle on another way out, a "Plan B" that would hitch her destiny to something other than the college catalogues arriving in her mailbox. Hull's narrative won third place in the Mayborn's Best American Newspaper Narrative Writing Contest.

John Branch's "Snowfall: The Avalanche at Tunnel Creek" is another powerful, place-driven narrative, set in a remote gorge called Tunnel Creek, part of the Cascade Mountains of Washington State. With a vertical descent of 3,000 feet through unobstructed views and soft powder, Tunnel Creek was the kind of place "that makes skiers giggle in glee," Branch wrote. But with its steep slopes, heavy snow with thin layers underneath of frost called surface hoar, Tunnel Creek also posed the ever-present risk of an avalanche.

And so when the cry went out from one of the skiers—AVALANCHE! —there wasn't much anyone could do. The avalanche quickly turned into a lethal locomotive, more than 1,000 cars long, barreling down the mountain at 70 m.p.h., plowing some of the 16 skiers and snowboarders beneath it.

Before the avalanche tore down Tunnel Creek, though, Branch built suspense. With reports of heavy snow falling on the mountain the night before, the skiers and snowboarders ascended it. "Each snowflake added to the depth, and each snowflake added to the weight," Branch writes. "It might take a million snowflakes for a skier to notice the difference. It might just take one for a mountain to move."

In sorting through the aftermath of the disaster, trying to make sense of it, Branch also discovered a universal truth about survival from interviewing the survivors. "As with other survivors, the quarrel with their own guilt began immediately," he wrote, "the first sign that avalanches swallow more lives than just the ones buried beneath the snow."

The survivors, all professional skiers and snowboarders, "wondered how so many smart, experienced people could make the types of decisions that turned complex, rich, enviable lives into a growing stack of statistics."

"Snowfall" was a runner-up in the Best American Newspaper Narrative Writing Contest, but no consolation is necessary. It won the Pulitzer Prize in feature writing in 2012.

Mark Johnson's "I Boy" is a provocative narrative that enables us to do what Scott Russell Sanders says many great stories do: "See through the eyes of other people," in this case, a two-year-old girl who sees herself as a boy. We watch Isabella ramming her baby carriage through her house like a race car, and observe other boy-like behavior. We read that she prefers Spider-Man cars, football, fire engines and tool benches to dolls.

At age four, Isabella's mother decides to take her to a stylist and saw her daughter's smile get bigger and bigger as her hair got shorter and shorter. Her mother decides it's time to call Isabella Izzy. "I Boy" offers readers what only great stories can do: to "reach across the rifts" of gender, as Sanders puts it, and actually feel the "experience of the other."

Dan Barry's "Donna's Diner" opens with Ike Maxwell shouting across a street in Elyria, Ohio, with "urgent intent," though no one is town seems to know or even care what he is shouting. "Dynamite Ike," an old high school football star, suffered multiple skull injuries when he was beaten on the head with a baseball bat 30 years ago and was later shot and seriously wounded. Ever since, he's been wandering the streets of this downtrodden town, "his shouts echoing off the ancient buildings," Barry writes.

But if you think this sounds like a tale about a favorite son's hard fall from stardom to the streets, think again. It's the compelling story of a community's sense of kinship, or the lack of it, at least when it comes to a deranged black man.

Ike Maxwell was "one of the most dominant athletes the city had ever known." He was an All-American, All-Ohio and winner of the Golden Helmet for being the best football player and student in Lorain County. Ike donated his Golden Helmet trophy to Elyria High School. Yet he was never inducted into the Elyria Hall of Fame or had a ballpark or a major roadway named after him. Town fathers blamed Ike's "erratic behavior" and lack of "moral character" for the snub.

Was that it? Barry's narrative, rife with irony and paradox, contains an important universal truth: racism is more nuanced now, more subtle, yet every bit as pernicious to a community's bonds of kinship as blows with a baseball bat are to the head.

Louis Hansen's "The Girl Who Took Down the Gang" pulls back the curtain of a violent subculture to reveal how a teenage tomboy in a new city was easily lured into a gang of criminals and murderers, the Bounty Hunter Bloods. The gang rituals, the coded language and shared weed gave 17-year-old Skyler Hayward a sense of belonging she hadn't known before.

But when her gang robbed three Navy sailors at a Norfolk, VA, parking lot, beat them with a gun, and killed one of them, Hayward faced a decision: To tell prosecutors what happened or lie. Either way, she was going to prison for her role in the murder. But if she testified against her Bounty Hunter Bloods brothers and sisters, the gang promised they'd slit her throat the first time they had a chance, inside or outside her cell.

She pleaded guilty to murder, testified against her fellow gang members and was sent to prison, living in solitary confinement for her own protection and writing lyrics about her loneliness and fear of violent death. "I'm so lonely it's alarming/I need people surround me/Oh no shelter for what's coming/It's my past and you must flee."

"The Girl Who Took Down the Gang" offers us another example of the power of storytelling: Showing us the consequences of our actions, but also the road to redemption. After five years behind bars, Hayward was released from prison, got a full-time job and an apartment and is now planning to attend college.

Rosalind Bentley's "The Nation's Poet" opens with a poetry reading in the Library of Congress. Natasha Trethewey is reading a brutal poem about the Ku Klux Klan burning a cross in her family's yard in Mississippi. America's newly crowned Poet Laureate fervently believes poetry can help us make sense of history—"why it still haunts us in our most intimate relationships with each other, but also in our political decisions."

Her quest is to make us care about poetry as much as she does, to appreciate how verse can illuminate neglected bits of history, allowing us to see the marginalized and the forgotten in a new light. "The Nation's Poet" points to yet another power of story: to educate our desires. Trethewey says poetry can teach us to be more understanding, more caring, more sympathetic toward neglected members of our society, especially when it's presented from their point of view. Even if we don't fall in love with poetry, "The Nation's Poet" coaxes us toward a higher calling: to pay attention to the forgotten heroes and heroines of history.

Monica Rhor's "Young Houstonians Go from Homelessness to College" is at its heart a fresh iteration of the resurrection story. Two teenagers and their families couldn't pay their rent, were cast out of their homes into the streets of Houston and ended up huddled on the floor of a grimy, cramped shelter sleeping next to 300 strangers. "The whole world, it seemed, had turned against them," Rhor writes. The two spent most nights sobbing about "the houses they lost, the proms they wouldn't attend, the colleges they couldn't afford."

With their world in tatters, Rhor offered her readers hope in the midst of the teens' hopelessness: "What they didn't yet know was that, sometimes, falling into shadow will lead you to the light."

That light came from Hope for Youth, a ministry for teens grappling with poverty, homelessness and hard times. It was there that Tiara met Courtney. They became instant friends, sharing their faith and encouraging each other not to give up. Hope for Youth "caught them as they were falling and led them to each other," Rhor writes.

Rhor's narrative takes readers through the teenagers' difficult quest. It's like "climbing up a crumbling mountain," but after a number of setbacks, Tiara and Courtney find solid footing and light that "edges out the darkness."

Scripture—that ancient narrative full of wisdom—reminds us in story after story that faith conquers all obstacles. Rhor's narrative embraces that Biblical belief in her story of homelessness and resurrection. "Homelessness doesn't have to last forever," she writes.

Martin Kuz's taut and terrifying narrative recounts a 60-second firefight in a dusty Afghanistan alley where two American soldiers, penned in with bullets pelting down from high above, face certain death. Bullets whirl, chewing up the walls in the alley and ripping through the soldiers, knocking them to the dirt.

Then a grenade lands on a mound of rock a few feet in front of them, clinking and tumbling in their direction. One of the soldiers covers the other, "their faces almost touching," Kuz writes. Silent seconds become deafening. One of the soldiers opens his eyes. "Where am I," he wonders. "Am I dead? Alive?"

That "everlasting minute" still lives on in the soldiers. But for us readers, far removed from death's ever-present grip on soldiers from both sides of the conflict, Kuz's story destroys the abstraction of war and the proximity of death faced each day on the battlefield.

"Soldiers Recount 60-Second Attack that Left Them Reflecting on Life and Death" offers a close encounter with the horrors of war that shatters our comfort zone and allows us, perhaps for the first time, to experience the reality of war like never before.

***

Taken together, this collection of the Best American Newspaper Narratives of 2012 is like a searchlight in the dark, illuminating the great mysteries and conundrums of the human condition. I hope that in reading the collection you'll come to the same conclusion I did: That your story and my story and all the stories in the collection are part of each other's story—one vast story about what it means to be human.

ACKNOWLEDGMENTS

The Mayborn Literary Nonfiction Conference has become a kind of Mecca for narrative nonfiction writing in America.

Over the past 10 years, the Mayborn has conducted writing contests and workshops to encourage journalists and nonfiction authors across the country to produce "original" nonfiction literature in the form of reported narratives, personal essays and book manuscripts. The Mayborn's writing contests are now attracting writers from around the country in search of new literary plateaus—staff writers for *The New York Times* and the *Atlanta Journal-Constitution*, freelancers for *GQ* and *Outside* magazine, and other journalists and authors dedicated to the narrative craft.

And we've awarded major cash awards and publishing opportunities in our literary anthology, *Ten Spurs*, for the ten "best of the best" submissions to the Mayborn. Literary agents and publishers have taken notice. Robert Atwan named *Ten Spurs, Vol. 4,* a "notable special issue" in his nationally acclaimed anthology, *2011 Best American Essays*.

Now, you're holding in your hands a new anthology, aptly named *The Best American Newspapers of 2012.* It grew out of the vision of Jim Moroney, publisher of *The Dallas Morning News*, who urged us to launch a writing contest for narratives previously published in the nation's dailies. He even offered to fund it. How could we say no?

The contest was a smashing success. Nearly every major daily in America participated. First-place winner was Eli Saslow, a national enterprise writer for the *Washington Post* for "Life of a Salesman." Saslow received $5,000 and free registration to attend last year's conference. "It's an honor to be recognized along with some of the writers I admire," Saslow said. "It's also heartening to see evidence of so many newspapers supporting narrative journalism." Saslow also was a finalist for the Pulitzer Prize in feature writing.

Second place and $2,000 went to Kelley Benham of the *Tampa Bay Times* for "Never Let Go," an emotionally wrought narrative about the birth of her daughter, Juniper, born more than 12 weeks premature. Benham was also a finalist for the Pulitzer Prize in feature writing in 2012, and she and her husband, Tom French, were presenters at our last conference.

Third place and $1,000 went to the *Post*'s Anne Hull for "Breaking Free," about a teenage girl's climb out of poverty. "These awards reflect not only the extraordinary gifts of Eli Saslow and Anne Hull but also the *Washington Post*'s unwavering commitment to ambitious narrative journalism," said Kevin Merida, the managing editor of the *Washington Post*.

Our judges selected three runners-up and four notable narratives for publication in this anthology, *The Best American Newspaper Narratives of 2012*. The runners-up were John Branch of *The New York Times* for "Snow Fall: The Avalanche at Tunnel Creek"; Dan Barry of *The New York Times* for "Donna's Diner"; and Rosalind Bentley of *The Atlanta Journal-Constitution* for "The Nation's Poet."

Four "notable narratives" were also selected by our judges: Mark Johnson, a Pulitzer Prize-winning writer for the *Milwaukee Journal Sentinel*, for "I Boy"; Monica Rhor of the *Houston Chronicle* for "Young Houstonians Go from Homelessness to College"; Louis Hansen of *The Virginian-Pilot* for "Girl Who Took Down a Gang"; and Martin Kuz, formerly of *Stars and Stripes*, for "Soldiers Recount Attack."

"With the focus on narrative journalism that these awards represent," said Moroney, the *Dallas Morning News* publisher, "we hope they will encourage more compelling, important and interesting narrative stories that attract and retain subscribers."

A few minutes spent with the dazzling prose and reportage represented inside *The Best American Newspaper Narratives of 2012* should remove any doubt that Jim's hope will be realized. As you read the stories in this compendium, I hope you'll agree that our highly acclaimed journalists and authors who spent weeks reading, evaluating and finally selecting the 10 best narrative submissions pouring in from around the country gave us a collection of stories that we'll want to turn to over and over again for years to come.

Our contest judges were Maria Carrillo, managing editor at *The Virginian-Pilot* in Norfolk; Roy Peter Clark, a former dean at the Poynter Institute; Roger Thurow, a former foreign correspondent for *The Wall Street Journal*; Michele Weldon, assistant professor of journalism at Northwestern University; and Mike Wilson, the former managing editor of *The Tampa Bay Times*. Their full bios appear nearby.

Publication of *The Best American Newspaper Narratives of 2012*, as well as an ebook version, was made possible by the Vick Family Foundation. Fran Vick and her family have been long-time friends and supporters of the Mayborn Conference and UNT Press, and we are deeply grateful to them. We also owe a debt of gratitude to Eric Nishimoto, an award-winning writer and illustrator who designed the eye-popping cover to this year's edition, and to Karen DeVinney, assistant director/managing editor of UNT Press, who edited the collection with competency and patience with a writer-in-residence who kept missing deadlines. And finally, to Ron Chrisman, the director of UNT Press, who deserves our accolades for his commitment to publishing extraordinary "literary nonfiction" in all its forms to enrich the lives of readers.

LIFE OF A SALESMAN

THE WASHINGTON POST

OCTOBER 7, 2012, SUNDAY SUBURBAN EDITION

By Eli Saslow

He had always managed to find optimism in even the worst circumstances, and here was another chance: a heat advisory, 98 degrees and
rising at 11 a.m., the hottest day of the year yet.

"Thank you," said Frank Firetti, 54, as he walked out of his Manassas
office into a blast of humidity in early June. "Thank you," he said again.
"What a perfect day to sell a pool."

He opened the trunk of his 2004 Toyota compact and changed into his
selling outfit of slacks, a yellow polo and a silver wristwatch. He rubbed
lotion on his face and sifted through six pairs of shoes before grabbing
his Dockside loafers. His goal was to arrive at a customer's house looking
"out of the catalogue," he said—no traces of mud on his feet, no worry
lines carved into his forehead, no indication whatsoever that sales at Blue
Haven Pools had been plummeting for five years running and that a staff
of 24 full-timers had dwindled to six.

His job was to stand with customers in their back yards, suntanned and smiling, and look beyond the problems of the past several years to see the opportunities in every suburban cul-de-sac. How about a pool and a sauna next to the patio? Or a custom waterfall near the property line?

"The possibilities here are as big as you can dream them," he liked to tell customers, gesturing at their yards.

In a country built on optimism, Frank Firetti was the most optimistic character of all: the American salesman—if not the architect of the American dream then at least its most time-honored promoter. He believed that you could envision something and then own it, that what you had now was never as good as what you would have next. Since the country was founded, it had climbed ever upward on the spirit of people like him, on their vision, on their willpower, on their capitalism. But now, when he traveled from house to house to sell his monuments to American success, he sensed that spirit waning.

Most people believed the country was headed in the wrong direction. Fewer trusted banks, employers or government. Two presidential campaigns were bombarding his swing state of Virginia with messages about a beleaguered middle class and an endangered American dream.

He had been taught that success in the United States was as simple as choosing it, and that one man's hard work and ambition mattered more than elections in Washington or whims on Wall Street. His grandfather had taken a boat from Italy to Ellis Island and become a brick mason who helped build a state capitol. His father had started five businesses, each bigger than the last, until the profits paid for 10 acres in Virginia and a stable for a racehorse. He had nieces who graduated from college, a brother who lived in a mansion and a Filipina wife who was in the process of becoming a U.S. citizen.

The promise of America was embedded in the Firetti family story.

But lately Frank had begun to see fissures in that story, signs of the anxiety and doubt that had reconfigured so much of the country. The economic morass of the past five years had downsized his business, diminished his retirement savings and devalued his house. Now the effects were threatening to become psychological, nibbling closer and closer at the corners of his self-worth and his optimism.

As the summer of 2012 began, he and his family had much more at stake than swimming-pool sales or even the survival of their business. In question now was the conviction at the heart of an American family—that the future was theirs to control.

His brother had begun saying the world felt like a "tinderbox, ready to explode." His father, the co-owner of their Blue Haven Pools franchise, was speaking of this election in the most critical terms, telling Frank that "the country as we know it is as good as gone without a change." His 19-year-old son had begun building up his savings account, living in Frank's basement and studying economics at the nearby community college, in part because he hoped there would still be a business for him to inherit.

Frank, meanwhile, continued to believe the answer to his future was always waiting on the next sales call, inside the door of the next house. Always the next house.

"Just got to close this one," he said now, driving his car toward the first sales call of the day, a noon appointment in Arlington County. "Close one and we'll be doing okay."

He loved being in the car, the one place that was his alone, where he could fortify himself against stress and negativity. There was Motrin in the center console for his headaches, hand sanitizer for germs and four empty bags of pistachios, because cracking shells occupied his hands and quieted his mind. There was classic rock on the radio, because he had changed the station when the host of his favorite conservative talk show started dissecting the economy, a word Frank couldn't stand to say or hear, because he had come to equate it with "an excuse for failure," he said.

There was a Bible open on the back seat, because having it there occasionally helped seal the deal with a religious customer, but mostly because Frank was an ardent believer who liked to read and annotate the book when his faith needed restoration.

He pulled up to a mini-mansion and parked in the shade, leaving the air conditioning running while he reviewed the customer's file. Four or five years ago, sales appointments had been his favorite part of the job. He was a former construction worker who knew how to build the pools he sold. There were other salesmen who rushed through their pitches and then pulled out a contract, but Frank liked to savor those first few hours in a customer's house, when everything seemed possible and he could sit with a sketch pad and interpret someone's vision.

His designs occasionally went over budget, but few customers seemed to mind. They could rely on equity in their homes and banks that were eager to loan.

"Selling is winning," he liked to say.

But now the wins came much less frequently, and customers wanted to talk more about warranties and payment plans. Many of them owed more on their mortgages than their homes were worth, and most banks considered it too risky to lend tens of thousands of dollars for a swimming pool.

Frank had tried to compensate by lowering his prices and improving the quality of his work, raising Blue Haven's rating with the Better Business Bureau from an F under previous ownership to an A-minus. He had taped a copy of a Native American poem about fearlessness to the first page of his appointment book. He had also taken to repeating an aphorism, a company goal that sounded more like a prayer when he said it now, as he stepped out of his car onto the sidewalk.

"This will be a good business if we can sell a hundred pools this year," he said.

"A hundred pools," he said again. Then he walked up the driveway and knocked on the door.

***

Frank's wife attributed his successes to talent, and his brother jokingly credited luck, but the truth was that Frank possessed the single quality most central to American achievement. "You've got to have that drive," he said, and he always had. That's how a mediocre high school student turned himself into a restaurant manager, and how a restaurant manager became a chief building engineer, and how a building engineer became a salesman for a Virginia moving company making $80,000 on straight commission.

He recognized opportunities and then seized them, never dwelling for too long on fears or self-doubts. He moved from one career to the next on a steady journey upward, pausing just long enough to hang a sign in the office that read, "God Bless America."

So, when his father asked if he wanted to tag along to a convention for swimming-pool salesmen in February of 2006 just to learn what the business was like, Frank answered the way he always had when a new opportunity arose.

"You bet," he said.

That's how he ended up at the Sheraton in Dallas with hundreds of other salesmen from 80 Blue Haven franchises across the country. His father, Sal Firetti, had recently joined Blue Haven as a salesman, and they spent three days spoiling themselves on the corporate expense account. It had been a record year for pool sales; there was all-you-could-eat prime rib at lunch and a specialized phone booth called a "money machine," set up in the lobby, where fans blew $20 bills and employees got 15 seconds each to step inside and stuff their shirts. Frank met two salesmen from the Manassas office, Dennis and Ted, who wore Hawaiian shirts and told stories about making $200,000 a year and traveling to the Bahamas on a company-paid cruise for salesmen who sold 42 pools or more.

"Greed on display," Frank called it, and he wanted in. He joined Blue Haven as a salesman within a year. He and his father bought the franchise in Manassas shortly thereafter. Sal was nearing 70, and he wanted to buy one more business as a legacy for the grandkids. Frank was nearing 50, and he wanted to transition from working for companies to helping run one. It was the next step up in what seemed to him like the classic American narrative. The Firetti men agreed to manage the business together, bonded by a philosophy.

"Go big or go home," Frank said.

Now, on a Tuesday morning in late June, Frank walked into the company that had become his own. Ted and his Hawaiian shirts were gone, retired to Florida. Dennis was selling for a competitor. His father was back in the hospital because of complications from an illness that left him chronically fatigued, so now Frank was mostly in charge of Blue Haven by himself. He didn't have a lot of money in the bank. After six years selling pools, he had yet to qualify for the company's annual cruise. "One guy selling 40 pools?" he said, shaking his head. "These days, they could fit that group into a canoe."

"Good morning," he said now, stepping into the office. "Anybody up here?"

His voice broke the silence and echoed off the walls. The office, once cramped with 24 employees, now felt like a mausoleum on a dead-end road in an industrial park. There were empty desks and scattered customer thank-you notes from the boom years. There was still his stepmother, a former teacher who had taught herself to keep the books. There was his earnest 16-year-old nephew, helping out for the summer in mesh shorts and untied sneakers. There was his son, Tyler, down in the basement warehouse bumping his head to rap music on an iPod and taking inventory of what supplies they had left.

Frank walked into his corner office and closed the door. He had been increasing his hours even as business slowed, believing he could work his way out by punching numbers into his oversize calculator and compiling photo albums to showcase the pools he built. The phone affixed to his hip rang every few minutes, although too few of the calls came from customers.

His father called on his way home from the hospital: Try lowering the prices again, he said.

His brother called: Hire some staff, he said. Take some risks. You're sitting on a gold mine. "A damn gold mine!"

Now there was a knock on his office door. "Yep," Frank said, and in walked Scott, his construction manager and most loyal employee. Scott was a talented builder who had worked for other pool companies, but he had stuck with Blue Haven through the downturn because he believed in the company's work. Even as its annual business dipped from 400 pools to a hundred, Frank had never asked Scott to build with cheaper materials or shortchange customer warranties.

"We've got a bit of a problem," Scott said. A storm had caused damage to one of their pools still under warranty, and it would require a few hundred dollars to fix.

"Does anything ever go right?" Frank asked. He looked up from his desk and smiled.

"Not lately," Scott said.

They stood together for a moment in the quiet office. When his family bought Blue Haven, Frank had vowed to take care of his employees. He wanted to start a profit-sharing plan and celebrate good years by taking the entire staff to the Bahamas. But now Scott hadn't taken a decent vacation in two years, and he had started cleaning pools to make ends meet. He had briefly considered leaving the business to work for the government.

"You ever think about doing something else?" Scott asked.

"Sure," Frank said. "Yesterday, day before, day before that. But deep down I still believe it will get good."

"A hundred pools?" Scott said. He had heard the refrain.

"Maybe 75, even 80," Frank said. "If we can do that, we'll all be doing real good."

***

At first, swimming pools were just another product that he sold: $40,000-to-$200,000 retail price; several thousand pounds of concrete followed by 30,000 gallons of water; a two-month construction headache for 6 percent commission.

But the more he learned about pools, the more he found them representative of something larger. They were carvings etched into back yards as a mark of ascent, commemorating a customer's arrival in the upper middle class. They were a signal: You had a pool, you were an American somebody. Frank loved to visit his construction sites, exchange his few words of Spanish with the crew and then patrol the area with a digital camera. The crews sometimes found it peculiar, but Frank didn't care. He wrote into each contract that he was allowed to take pictures and chronicle his creation. A black hole in the earth became a smooth bowl of white-and-blue speckled plaster, filled with water so calm and pristine that it offered a promise. Here was a place of undisturbed relaxation, of aqua blue and sandstone, a monument to luxury that could be owned. He hung photos of his favorite pools in the office and brought others home to show his wife. He wanted one.

His sister already owned a pool, a custom model with two waterfalls and a hot tub that Frank had sold to her at a discounted cost.

His brother had purchased a few pools in his life before deciding it would be better to buy a house on the water.

His father had a pool on three acres in Purcellville, where he hosted family parties and cooked Italian meals on Sundays.

About a year after Frank started working for Blue Haven, he had decided to design a pool of his own. It would be his most ambitious creation yet—the biggest pool he had ever drawn, a concept he was sure nobody had thought of before. He drew a 1,200-square-foot pool with an island dotting the center and a lazy river wrapped around the perimeter.

"I'm going to lie on my back and float in circles all day." That was his plan.

Four years later, on a breezy evening in July, Frank came home to a townhouse in Purcellville sandwiched between two identical townhouses. It had been a promising day at work—one pool sold, another just waiting on county approval—and he cracked open a beer and grabbed a copy of his old drawing from the basement. His pool was still only a plan, stored alongside the yellowed schematics for a house he had hoped to build in Purcellville. He already owned the land, but their townhouse had declined in value and their money was tied up in Blue Haven. "Someday," he said.

He grabbed another beer and carried it out to the deck.

His son, Tyler, was already there, just back from his daily workout at the gym, and Frank sat across from him. His wife, Suzette, was inside packing for a trip to visit her family in the Philippines, and his 7-year-old daughter was dancing to music videos in the living room. It was just the two of them outside, father and son, drinking beer in a light breeze as the sun dipped toward the horizon. "Is there a better night than this?" Frank said, feeling wistful.

He began to talk about the things he wanted, his hallmarks of success in America: a Harley, a new camper, a family trip to Italy and that pool with the lazy river.

Tyler responded in turn by listing his own goals, which so many people in his father's generation had considered guarantees. "Stocks. Bonds. A house. A car," he said. He had been working double shifts as a waiter to boost his savings. He wanted to pay down his community college loans before transferring to a four-year college to finish his degree.

"Those are all good things," Frank said. "Smart. Real practical."

"You can't be too safe or too smart about money with the economy now," Tyler said. "I want to save up and make the smart investments."

"You'll make them," Frank said, nodding.

"I want to have that absolute stability," Tyler said.

"You'll have it."

They stayed out on the deck until the sun disappeared behind the townhouses. Frank went to bed just before midnight and awoke at 4. He always had been a sound sleeper, but lately he had been putting himself to bed with Tylenol PM and stirring awake to questions in the middle of the night. When had stability become the goal in America? What kind of dream was that? And in the economy of 2012, was it even attainable?

He had begun a habit of leaving his bedroom in the middle of the night without waking his wife. He would grab a blanket and walk out to a chair on the deck. It had become his favorite place to sleep. There was peace in the silence and perspective in the stars. There was comfort in the familiar churning sound of a swimming pool. It was a public one, located just across the street.

***

A few days later, Frank's father, Sal, came into work for the first time in weeks, taking the stairs up to the office two at a time, chest hair rising over his yellow Hawaiian shirt.

"Let's sell some pools," he said, clapping his hands.

He had gone to the hospital again the day before, and he had been too fatigued to leave home the day before that. But now here he was at 73, barking orders into his cellphone, hair slicked, feeling suddenly better.

"How we doing, Frank?" Sal said. "You good?"

It was a family habit not to allow for the possibility of any other answer.

"You bet," Frank said. "Real good."

Nothing reinforced his sense of possibility so much as seeing his father on a good day, shouting in Italian and marching around the office with the self-assurance of a man who had spent most of his life as a boss. Sal had started an alarm company, owned a hardware and appliance store and traveled regularly to Asia for an import business. His family loved to tell one story about his days as a salesman for Motorola, when he talked his way into an appointment with Redskins coach George Allen and then walked out 20 minutes later with a signed contract and a complimentary pair of season tickets. To his family, he had always been the best salesman of all.

Now his gravelly baritone filled the office as he called subcontractors and offered advice to Frank. They wrote down names of customers on a dry-erase board, and Frank booked sales appointments in his day planner. He had four customers on the verge of buying pools and 15 more who had expressed interest on the company's voice mail. Maybe his brother was right: Maybe they really could do millions. Maybe he could still hit a hundred. Now was the time to invest, to swing big, to hire a few more salespeople and call back some of those hesitant buyers for one more try. He picked up the phone and started dialing.

"Happy wife, happy life," he told one customer.

"Aren't you tired of baking in this heat?" he asked another.

Sal ordered pizza for lunch, and Frank joined him in the conference room. Sal loaded hot pepper flakes onto a slice and starting telling a story about a trip to Italy a decade earlier. He had been wandering around Ischia, an island off the coast of Naples, looking into their family ancestry when his guide led him to an apartment with a marble staircase worn from centuries of use. At the top of those stairs was a small apartment, and in that apartment was a friendly old woman who turned out to be a distant relative, and on her wall was a black-and-white picture of Sal's grandfather.

"Marble stairs worn in the middle," Sal said, shaking his head.

"And still standing," Frank said.

"Makes you feel like a part of something," Sal said.

"Something that lasts," Frank said.

They ate in silence for a minute, thinking about the decades of drive and ambition that had delivered their family to this office in Manassas. From Italy to the United States in 1911; from Firetto to Firetti during the chaos of processing at Ellis Island; from handcrafted marble steps to American brick masonry; from an apartment on a volcanic island to 10 acres in the rolling horse country of Virginia. The Firetti family narrative was the story of steady advance, of one generation after the next overcoming distance and circumstance to accomplish something greater.

Now it was left to Frank to outdo the past again, and something about that thought made the office feel small and quiet. He stood up from the table and rubbed his forehead. "Back to work," he said.

Sal returned to his office, sank into his chair and closed his eyes. "I'm exhausted," he said. And then, almost whispering: "Damn sickness." He stood up from his desk and walked over to see Frank.

"I'm going home," he said.

"What happened?" Frank said. "I thought you were doing good."

"La vecchiaia e una carogna," Sal said, repeating an Italian phrase that meant getting old involved nothing but pain.

"You know I hate it when you say that," Frank said.

"Ah, come on. I'm going to hell in a handbasket."

Frank winced. "Okay," he said. "Go get a little rest."

He watched his father ease down the steps, leaving him alone in the office. His glasses sat low on his nose and his shoulders slumped toward his desk. The phones had stopped ringing. The leads on the company voice mail sounded mostly like dead ends. There was a letter taped on the wall from Blue Haven's corporate office, sent a few months earlier. "Most offices have had to let go employees," it read. "Those sales reps still with Blue Haven represent the crème de la crème. Being in this elite group is an accomplishment in itself!"

He stood up from his desk and walked into the company's storage room, the place he went whenever his optimism began to feel misguided. There were cardboard boxes piled high on the shelves, each one filled with Blue Haven contracts from 2005, 2006 and 2007, great years for the American economy. Frank sat on a knee-high stool in the center of the room and reached for the closest box. The label read: "Last Name M, 2006," and inside were 42 swimming-pool contracts sold to a single letter in a single year.

He pulled out contracts and started to read the sale prices: "Sixty-two thousand," he said. "Eighty. Fifty-four. A hundred-and-twenty. Ninety-seven."

He reached for another box.

"Forty-two. Seventy-eight. Sixty-seven."

Quieter now.

"Fifty. Ninety-one. Can't you see? This place was mega."

He looked up and stared at the boxes stacked high on the walls, over-come by the evidence. What had come before was better than what he had now. Maybe, despite so much hard work and ambition, he couldn't do mega. Maybe, in the summer of 2012, all he could do was this:

"Fifty pools," he said, standing up from the stool. "Fifty pools and we'll be doing all right."

***

One night late in the summer, Frank carried a plate of leftovers and his laptop to the kitchen table so he could video-chat with Suzette, shortly after she arrived in the Philippines. She had traveled back to her home town of Dumaguete City six times in the decade since they married, but he had never gone. The flight cost $1,700, and a worthwhile trip across the world required more vacation time than Frank had taken in years.

Suzette appeared on his screen, and Frank saw the only view of the Philippines he had come to know: a whitewashed stucco wall, a kitchen chair and his wife holding coffee in her hand. It was 8 a.m. for her. The picture blurred and the volume faded out.

"What are you doing today?" Frank asked.

"What?" Suzette said, leaning closer to her computer.

"What are you doing today?" he yelled.

"Oh, we are still getting ready for the party."

It was the one-year anniversary of Suzette's mother's death, and she and her sisters had planned an event for 300. As usual, they had paid for all of it.

"Free dinner on the Firettis?" Frank said.

"What?" Suzette said.

She pointed to her ear, indicating a problem with the volume, but Frank wondered if she was choosing not to hear. She had spent almost $25,000 in the past three years to support relatives in the Philippines, and her frequent trips to Western Union had become a point of contention in an otherwise happy marriage.

The "Land of Money"—that was what Suzette's relatives sometimes called the United States. Her older sister had immigrated first on a temporary visa to do housework for a diplomat and then recommended Suzette for a similar job in 1988. She boarded a plane for the first time, traveled 38 hours and reunited with her sister at the airport. They stopped at Pizza Hut and drove to clean a house in the Washington suburbs. Five hours later, she had $80 in cash—the equivalent of a good month's wage in Dumaguete City.

Suzette had been working steadily ever since, caring for an autistic child and tidying houses in order to send $250 a month back to her family. News of her generosity had traveled quickly, and now, whenever Suzette came to the Philippines, she found dozens of people waiting outside her family's house hoping for a little help from the Land of Money. They saw the United States the same way she once had, as a place of endless opportunity, where even the cleaning ladies got rich. Now she knew better, but they didn't.

Frank looked at his wife on the computer screen and noticed her fingernails, each painted a different color. He had fallen for her at a barbecue a decade earlier, asking for her number and then calling the next day, but it had taken her a month to call back. She had confidence built during her years as a onetime beauty queen and member of an elite dance troupe. He had papers from a recent divorce and a temporary room in his father's house.

A few months into the relationship, Sal approached Suzette and asked what she thought about his son. "He has a kind heart," she told him. "He is a great father and a gentle man. It's not just the person he is now but the person he is becoming."

A decade later, he was still becoming. Frank sometimes wondered what Suzette's family thought when they wandered into view during these

Skype conversations, stopping to wave and look into his living room. Did they wonder why he didn't visit them? Why Suzette couldn't give away more?

Did they consider him a disappointment in the Land of Money?

It was a possibility too hard to discuss, especially now, on a computer connection across the world.

"I love you," Suzette said.

"I love you, too," Frank said.

The screen went dark, and he walked into the kitchen. He rifled through the fridge, finding only a leftover bratwurst. He opened the freezer and frowned. "Nothing good," he said. Suzette would be away for two more weeks. His father was back in the hospital. It was just him, alone with the responsibilities of his townhouse and his business.

He took out his appointment book and checked his schedule for the next day. "Pretty light," he said. He stared at the page and then began flipping ahead to the next week and the next month, looking for a sign of possibility before summer's end.

**

And then, out of nowhere, one came.

A couple stumbled onto Blue Haven's Web site, liked what they saw and invited Frank to their house. He dressed in his slacks and yellow polo and silver watch and drove to Oakton, where he parked in the shade and idled in the car. He read over the first lines of the Native American poem in his appointment book. He checked his hair in the rearview mirror and smiled at his reflection. "Selling is winning," he said.

A man greeted Frank in the driveway, wearing a white-collared shirt and cuff links, and led him into the living room.

"Beautiful house," Frank said, taking a seat across from the man and his wife. He pointed out the window to the back yard, shaded by 100-year-old trees. "And a beautiful place for a pool," he said.

"We've been thinking about a pool since 2007," the husband said. "We're tired of waiting for a perfect comeback that might never happen. We want to enjoy our money."

"We want that negative edge, that waterfall," the wife said.

"A one-of-a-kind pool," the husband said.

Frank reached into his pocket and grabbed a pencil. "An infinity edge, huh?" he said, beginning to sketch.

"With mood lighting," the wife said.

"Somewhere in the range of a hundred-and-twenty grand," the husband said.

Frank started to draw faster, sharpening the borders of the pool, grinning, nodding, bouncing his knee. "Okay," he said. "Okay! A one-of-a-kind pool."

They watched him sketch, and Frank let his imagination run. "An infinity edge," he said again, mostly for himself. Here were people with a dream that they trusted him to shape. Here was money and ambition. Here was a house in one of the richest neighborhoods in the country—a place built on American success. He shaded in the interior of the pool and handed the sketch to the wife.

"Beautiful," she said. And then, a few minutes later: "I like you, Frank."

"I trust you, Frank," the husband said. "We'll be in touch soon."

"I can't wait to hear," Frank said, beaming, sensing in his gut what would soon become contractual—the couple would buy a pool for $155,000, one of his biggest sales of the summer.

He walked out of the house to his car and turned up the classic rock on his radio. "Momentum," he said, drumming against the steering wheel. One big sale would surely lead to others. He called his father to share the news. "Could be a good August," he said. Selling was winning. The future was still his to control. He drove back to the office, pushing the speed limit, ready for the opportunities ahead.

***

And then he waited. And waited. The phones stayed quiet. His son and his nephew went back to school. His stepmother cut back on her hours. A subcontractor left early to spend the winter in Texas. August remained as slow as July, and as slow as June and May before that.

Frank sat alone in the office on Industrial Road at the end of the month and looked out the window. Out there, unemployment was near 8 percent, the presidential election was still a tossup and America remained unsettled. Another of his competitors was about to go under, and Frank wondered who might be next. The economy had turned business into a game of survival and sales into an exercise in humility. It had to get better. He was sure of it. But what if it didn't? If a salesman lost his optimism, what did that mean for everyone else?

He rubbed his hand over his eyes and picked up his calculator. Their landlord had agreed to halve the rent so long as they took care of the property, and now an afternoon shadow crept across overgrown grass, and weeds broke through the parking lot. Summer was ending, and soon it would be their slow season—a time to reckon with results.

They wouldn't be selling 100 pools.

Not 75.

Not 50.

"Just have to hold our breath and make it to spring," Frank said, still looking out the window, sounding resigned.

He heard a car pull into the parking lot and watched a man and a dog make their way to the front door. It was Blue Haven's former sales manager—a man who had trained Frank to sell pools and then left to start his own swimming-pool company when the business slowed. He climbed to the top of the stairs, and Frank greeted him at the landing and shook his hand.

"Quiet up here," the former sales manager said. "How's business?"

"Good, thanks," Frank said. He stood firm at the top of the stairs, holding the sales manager near the entrance to block his view of the rest of the office. Behind him, the dry-erase board of current projects was mostly empty. The only noise was the faint voice of Sean Hannity on the radio, dissecting the latest lackluster jobs report and what it meant for the presidential election.

The sales manager looked past Frank to the empty desks and the old thank-you notes on the wall.

"In the last seven weeks, I've done a million in business," the sales manager said, patting his dog on the head while he spoke. "It's not where it was, probably won't be in my lifetime. But it's something."

"Yep. It's coming around," Frank said. He took another step forward, moving the sales manager a few feet closer to the door.

"You're looking more and more like your dad every day," the sales manager said.

Frank smiled. "Good to see you."

The sales manager nodded and walked down the steps. When he reached the bottom, he stopped and turned around.

"Hey, Frank."

"Yeah."

"I'm looking to expand, you know. So, if things are hard, and if you ever get tired of being committed to this, just give me a call. We can figure out a deal."

Frank looked back at him for a long minute, mulling over the irony. The past five years had turned everything upside down, and now there was a salesman standing at his front door, feeding him lines, sensing an opportunity and offering a deal.

"You're treating me like a customer," Frank said.

He stepped closer to the stairs before he said what came next. Because even during this time of doubt and disappointment, there remained one conviction to which he was still clinging—a belief at the core of his optimism that he needed to make clear.

"I'm the salesman," he said.

NEVER LET GO

TAMPA BAY TIMES

DECEMBER 9, 12, 16, 2012

By Kelley Benham

When a baby is born at the edge of viability, which is the greater act of love: to save her, or to say goodbye?

PART ONE

Our baby came swirling into view in black and white, week after week, in the grainy wedge on the ultrasound monitor. First a dark featureless pool, then a tiny orb, then budding arms and legs and finally long fingers and a recognizable profile. Precisely on schedule, I felt her squirm and thump.

After years of grueling and unnatural fertility treatments, the promise of her unfolded easily.

We learned her gender in week 16, cataloged her anatomy in week 20. I scrubbed the baseboards in the spare bedroom and stopped buttoning my jeans. I tried to imagine her as a real child, in my hands and in my life.

I drew, in ballpoint pen, her cartoon outline on my skin—with big eyes, a sprout of hair, and an umbilical tether to my navel that made her look like a startled space walker. That was the extent to which I understood her: only in outline, the details waiting to be filled in.

Suddenly there was blood. Blood on my hands. Blood on a thin cotton hospital gown. Blood in red rivulets and blood in dark clumps. Bright beads of blood on the doctor's blue latex gloves. Blood in such startling quantity we could only imagine there was no life, no baby, not anymore.

My obstetrician looked stricken that day in March 2011 when he rushed into a triage room at Bayfront Medical Center. I clenched and vomited as he explained that our baby had no chance of surviving outside the womb —if she wasn't already gone. A tech tried for long minutes to summon a heartbeat on the monitor, searching every quadrant of my abdomen. I don't remember if we held our breath or gasped or spoke or sobbed. I remember only the frozen shock when a heartbeat flooded the room, a sound like a galloping horse.

In just a few hours, our baby had been lost and then found. On the monitor, she bobbed and floated in a pixelated haze. But next to her loomed a mysterious shape that had not been there two days before: a clot of blood the size of a fist, created as the placenta had begun to tear loose from my body. A nurse pumped drugs into an IV to stall the labor, and gradually they took a tenuous hold. But it was clear to everyone that the reprieve was temporary. My baby and I were coming apart.

A normal pregnancy lasts 40 weeks. I was only halfway there.

If the doctors had not intervened, my baby would have been a miscarriage. But the odds for her had not improved by much.

Early arrival kills more newborns than anything else, and complications from prematurity kill more babies in the first year than anything else.

Some babies are born so early they are beyond rescue. If a baby is born at or before the 22nd week, it is usually considered a miscarriage or a stillbirth. Almost no doctor will intervene, because there is nothing he or she can do.

Other babies ripen in the womb into the third trimester but arrive a little early. If a baby is born later than about 25 weeks, studies show that almost all doctors feel morally and legally obligated to try to save its life. Some preemies have serious medical problems, but most spend a few days or weeks in the hospital learning to breathe and eat and then they go home.

In between those scenarios is a zone between life and death, between viability and futility. If a baby is born after the 22nd week of pregnancy but before the 25th, not even the smartest doctors in the world can say what will happen to it. New technologies can sometimes keep these micropreemies alive, but many end up disabled, some catastrophically so. Whether to provide care to these infants is one of the fundamental controversies in neonatology.

Babies born at the edge of viability force us to debate the most difficult questions in medicine and in life. Who deserves to live, and at what cost? Who decides whether a life is worth saving, or worth living? When does a fetus become a human being, with its own rights? When does life begin?

About one in 750 babies arrives in that awful window of time, suspended between what is medically possible and what is morally right.

One of them was born on April 12, 2011, at Bayfront Medical Center. My daughter.

This summer I returned, not as a parent, but as a journalist, to the hospital where my daughter was born. I interviewed the people who took care of her about the scientific and ethical challenges of trying to save babies born so soon. I pored over her medical chart and read dozens of journal articles on extreme prematurity. I learned the things the doctors had been too kind to tell us, and the things I'd been too dazed to comprehend.

When the doctors stalled my labor, they gave us a slim measure of hope, but no assurances. Our baby could die quickly, could die slowly, could suffer needlessly, could live vegetatively. She could be broken in any pocket of her body or mind.

She would come squawking into the world unfinished and vulnerable. Conceived artificially, she would have to grow in an artificial womb. She would reveal to us the wonders of medicine and science, and the limits of those things. She would show us the ferocity of our most primal instincts.

A sci-fi baby in an engineered world, she'd teach me, against all possible odds, what it means to be a mom.

The Baby Place at Bayfront Medical Center is designed for celebrations. The rooms are private, with sleeping couches and flat screen TVs. Sliding panels obscure all evidence of the mess and peril of birth. Mothers are wheeled out holding fat drowsy newborns, dutiful dads follow with the balloons. Every time a baby is born, the loudspeaker carries the tinkling of a lullaby.

It's easy to pretend, in that cozy place, that all babies come wailing into the world pink and robust, and are bundled and hatted and handed to teary mothers and proud dads. But sometimes it doesn't go that way at all. That's why behind the sliding panels there are devices for oxygen, suction and epinephrine. That's why there's a morgue on the ground floor. That's why Bayfront's labor and delivery unit is actually housed across the street, inside All Children's Hospital. When a baby is born in trouble, as mine was bound to be, it is already in the place that cares for some of the sickest and most fragile children in the state.

After the day I almost lost the baby, the doctors made it clear that for now I had one purpose in life: Stay pregnant. In their calmest and firmest bedside voices the doctors said I had to make it another month to 24 weeks, loosely considered the limit of human viability outside the womb. Deliver earlier than that, and I would watch my baby struggle and die.

I lay still in bed and watched the calendar as my baby survived to 21 weeks, then 22. I checked in and out of the hospital twice, and then back in. I Googled images of half-formed babies. I bled and cramped. One tactless doctor made the situation plain when he tried to discharge me. "Your baby is not viable," he said, "so you might as well deliver at home."

By the 23rd week, I was taunted by that incessant lullaby on the hospital loudspeaker, a reminder of how natural this process was supposed to be. Nothing about it had been natural for me. To get this far had taken four years, $40,000, four in-vitro procedures, an egg donor, lawyers, counselors and contracts. Now my body was trying to spit out the baby we'd made. It felt like biological mutiny.

I stayed anchored to the hospital bed by a strap around my belly that charted the volcanic activity within on a computer monitor. The contractions came and went, and when they got bad enough, the doctors stalled the labor by elevating my feet above my head and flooding me with magnesium sulfate, which made me feel like my blood and skin were on fire. That's how I was—inverted, scalding—when doctors conceded the baby was coming soon, and a neonatologist visited to advise my husband and me of what lay ahead.

Dr. Aaron Germain was thin and kind, with a look of constant worry. I viewed him as an ambassador from the Land of Sick Babies, a place I could not imagine.

He told us he knew how badly we wanted our child, and an army of specialists with the most advanced technology was ready upstairs to try to save her life. But we needed to decide whether saving her was what we really wanted. The effort would require months of aggressive intervention, and could leave us with a child who was alive, but very damaged.

Few doctors would insist on intervening. The choice was ours to make.

He went through the list of possible calamities, each with its own initials. IVH, PVL, RDS, CLD, ROP, CP. The magnesium sulfate burned through me, sucking the will from every cell. Blood in the brain. Hole in the heart. Respiratory distress. Chronic lung disease. Ventilator. Wheelchair. Blind. Deaf. Developmental delays. Autism. Seizures. Cerebral palsy.

Every part of her was underdeveloped, fragile and weak. Every treatment would exact a toll. She might live, but she would likely have, to use the medical term, profound morbidities.

Odds she would die, no matter how hard they tried: better than half.

Odds she would die or be profoundly disabled: 68 percent.

Odds she would die or be at least moderately disabled: 80 percent.

There was a 20 percent chance she could live and be reasonably okay. I pictured her in the slow class at school, battling asthma or peering through thick glasses. We would buy her pink sparkly ones and tell her they were cool.

I contemplated that figure: 20 percent. It didn't seem hopeless. Then again, imagine a revolver with five chambers. Now put four bullets in it and play Russian roulette. Would we bet on a 20 percent chance if losing might mean losing everything we cared about? Would we torture our baby with aggressive treatment just so she could live out her life in a nursing home or on a ventilator? Would we lose our house? Would our marriage fall apart?

Dr. Germain gamely counseled us as we searched for loopholes in the statistics. Girls do better than boys, he said, but white babies like ours fare worse than black babies. Our daughter would be delivered by C-section so her body didn't get mangled in the birth canal, and I would be injected with steroids before she was born to strengthen her lungs. But the figures the doctor had given us already accounted for those advantages.

But what were the odds, we wanted to know, for a middle-class girl baby with good parents, who sing songs and read stories? With two big brothers and aunts and uncles and a friendly, big-eared dog? The baby who slumbered inside me, her heartbeat galloping along over the speakers, reminding us that she was perfectly fine in there, and safe, and how wrong it was that soon she would be wrenched into the bright, cold air, and made to breathe?

Dr. Germain spoke softly and didn't rush. I wanted to shake him and his probabilities, to make him yelp and tell us what to do.

He just couldn't say. The answers we wanted weren't in the data.

"The statistics don't matter," he said, "until they happen to you."

What echoed in my head was something Dr. Germain never said: Saving her might be the most selfish act in the world.

After the doctor left, my husband sat on the edge of the bed and held my hand as we tried to work our way toward a decision. I started with shedding my expectations. We were a family of high achievers. My husband, Tom French, was a Pulitzer Prize-winning writer. His two sons, Nat and Sam, were salutatorian and valedictorian, respectively, at Gibbs High. Now they were off at college. We had envisioned a similar path for our daughter— horseback riding, piano lessons and the dean's list. All that was gone now, and we grappled with the fundamentals. Would we try to keep her alive? If she lived, would she walk or talk? Would she one day give us a look that said, Why did you put me through this?

People always ask me if I prayed. I prayed the way people in foxholes are said to pray. I prayed with every thought and every breath. And I prayed with the certainty that I had no business praying, that I hadn't earned the right. I'd never been religious. Worse, I knew we had defied the natural order in our determination to have a child. Through so many in-vitro procedures, with so many tests and needles and vials of drugs, we'd created life in a petri dish. To be given a child just long enough to watch her die felt like punishment for our hubris.

I was crying when I asked Tom, "Did we want her too much?"

I don't remember sleeping that night. As dawn crept closer, we both swallowed the thing we couldn't say. I knew once I said it our baby would be gone, and we'd be the parents who'd turned our backs. Tom climbed in next to me on the skinny bed and wrapped his arms around me and all of the wires as best he could.

"I don't know how to do this," he said.

Our baby's heart kept beating. I held out my iPhone and used its voice recorder to capture the sound, in case it was the only evidence of my daughter I would ever have.

I'm here, it seemed to be telling us. I'm still here.

Google was of no use. The research was confusing and out of date. The blogs and news sites trumpeted miracle babies but offered little nuance or detail. Nothing we read reflected the agony and complexity of the situation we faced.

The next day, a second counselor arrived from the neonatal intensive care unit. Nurse practitioner Diane Loisel found us still choking on indecision and grief.

Diane had a relaxed, no-makeup look, a contrast to the crisp, professional bearing of the neonatologist. Given the stakes, I thought, could we get another doctor in here? As soon as she started to talk, I felt foolish. She was so straightforward and so patient, it was clear that her only priority was our baby.

Diane told us she had worked with small and sick babies for 30 years. When she started, 23 weekers never made it out of the delivery room. Any baby born weighing less than 1,000 grams—about 2 pounds—was considered not viable and allowed to die. But now science had advanced, raising new questions for everybody.

Some parents insisted the doctors do everything possible, and then insisted on the impossible too. Diane told us it sometimes made her angry to see tiny babies subjected to futile intervention, to see them go into nursing homes or to families ill equipped to care for them. The more educated parents asked more questions, considered quality of life. Diane often wondered if asking parents to make such life-and-death decisions was cruel.

When it came to babies born at 23 weeks, research showed, there was little consensus from one hospital to the next or even among doctors working the same shift in the same unit.

Some were born limp and blue, and some came out pink and crying. In those first hours and days, much could be revealed. And there was a window of time, while the baby was on a ventilator and still very fragile, when doctors and families could reverse course and withdraw life support.

"You don't have to decide right now," she said. "It's a process."

She seemed to be offering an escape from the torment we had suffered all night. Enough of the unbearable coin toss. We could let them intervene and see how it went. If our baby was born too weak, we could decide later to let her go.

"We don't want her to suffer," Tom said. "But we want our baby to have a chance."

As Diane headed back to the NICU, she told me later, she knew she had changed everything. She also knew that once a mother had seen her baby for the first time, there often was no turning back. She hoped we wouldn't blame her for the rest of our lives.

Another day went by. I imagined my baby gathering a few more air sacs in her budding lungs, a few more ripples in her developing brain. Every hour was crucial, but how many would be enough?

Tom and I discovered it was impossible to stay miserable around the clock. We amused ourselves by speculating about the romantic lives of the doctors and nurses. One doctor looked like a lost Kennedy. Another one

—I called him Dimples—kept the nurses laughing. We could hear them out in the hall. Our favorite was a glossy-haired nurse we called Cupcake who wore Grey's Anatomy label scrubs. I imagined all of them screwing in supply closets and gossiping at the nurses' station. One of the doctors, while sketching a diagram of the untenable situation in my uterus, asked if I had any questions.

"Just one," I said. "Is it me or are the people on this floor unusually hot?"

"Yes," he said, "and thank God for it."

All of these people had been between my legs, and I was too wrecked to care. The absurdity of it made me laugh, even though laughter was discouraged while on bed rest.

That afternoon we watched DVDs and allowed ourselves to hope the doctors were wrong and we would make it another week. As soon as the sky darkened outside the window, I tried to sleep, to make the day end before anything could ruin it.

Still tethered like Gulliver by IVs and wires, I shifted left, then back to the right. Adjusted the bed up and back down. Stole my husband's pillow and asked the nurse for extra blankets. A vague sense of unease settled in and I shut my eyes and willed it away. The monitor registered no unusual activity.

When the nurse came in for yet another blood pressure, I told her I felt strange.

Constipation, she said.

At first it was uncomfortable. Then it started to hurt. The monitor mocked me with its refusal to acknowledge what I was feeling. I kept moving the straps around, trying to pick up the signal, then gave up and tossed them all off. I paced the floor, clutching an IV pole, setting off alarms at the nurse's desk.

I had a prescription for morphine, but the nurse stuck to her constipation theory and refused to give me any pain relief at all. I cramped for hours until she sent my husband on a 2 a.m. trek through St. Petersburg in search of prune juice. By the time Tom returned with a 64-ounce bottle, I was screaming on the bathroom floor.

The pain was sharp and low and I could feel the baby kicking with both feet like a mule trying to take down a barn door. "Please," I told the baby. "Be still."

The nurse appeared in the doorway. "What would it feel like if there were feet coming out of me?" I asked her. "Because that's what this feels like."

"No, honey," she assured me. "That's not what's happening."

A doctor finally checked just before dawn. I was sobbing and gulping air. I asked him if he could put me in a coma, and make it all stop, and wake me up in a couple of months when the baby was bigger. Or maybe he could sew me shut. Or hang me upside down. He pulled on his gloves and told me to be still and to breathe.

"Please be careful please be careful please be careful." I couldn't get my breath. "Please be careful."

He reached in and felt the baby's feet, just where I knew he would find them.

A second doctor confirmed it. "We have to go now," she said.

We'd made it 23 weeks and six days.

I watched the ceiling roll by as nurses whisked me on my hospital bed to Operating Room 4. Doctors debated whether there was time for anesthesia, then someone rolled me over and put a needle in my spine and the pain washed away.

If I'd been able to sit up and look around, I would have seen a group from the NICU, called the Stork Team, preparing to stabilize the baby in a room next to the O.R.

Gwen Newton was the Stork Team nurse that day. She described it all for me later. She said most mornings, she needs a good jolt of coffee to get going. But today, all it took was a look at her assignment sheet: 23 weeker.

When she was pregnant with her son, she said, she had nightmares that he was born at 23 weeks.

She readied a mobile incubator that would keep the baby warm and monitored on the short ride to the NICU. She made a nest of blankets and spread a pillowcase over it to catch the blood.

The baby's arm would be so small she'd use a rubber band for a tourniquet. She got out a No. 1 blood pressure cuff, small enough to fit around her finger. She set the warmer to 37 degrees Celsius, laid out catheters for IVs and wires for monitors. She drew a mixture of sugar and dextrose in a 60 mL syringe—a snack to get the baby started. And she drew 1.4 mL of an artificial lung surfactant—a milky mix of fats and proteins that would help prevent the baby's sticky lungs from collapsing.

A respiratory technician was prepping the ventilator and a neonatologist and a nurse practitioner were studying the chart. When Gwen had everything ready, she stepped to the doorway to watch the C-section.

Some of what happened next would be out of her control. Some babies came out fighting and some did not. You never know what's coming out of that belly, she thought.

I felt a sickening tug. I knew that we were two separate people now.

"She's kicking," Tom said. He was peering over the surgical drape at the gaping red meat of my abdomen, and at the creature that had just emerged from it. Someone said she cried, but I didn't hear it. I tasted prune vomit in my mouth.

Pretty soon someone slipped a piece of paper in front of me, and an ink pad, and asked for a fingerprint. On the paper were two still-wet footprints, each an inch and a half long. Startling evidence that she was here.

"My baby," I kept saying, "my baby, my baby."

Gwen took the tiny blood-spotted bundle from the delivery nurse. She unwrapped her, laid her on heat packs, and slipped her into a plastic bag up to her neck to help prevent heat and fluid loss. Gwen rubbed and dried her like a mother cat roughs up a kitten, but more gently, so as not to tear her skin. The baby was dusky blue, then dark red. Gwen pinched the tiny greenish umbilical cord between her thumb and forefinger and felt it throb. She counted 17 beats in six seconds.

"Heart rate is 170," she called out. It was strong, a good sign.

The baby was trying to breathe but her lungs were not ready and her muscles were weak. Through the stethoscope her breathing sounded squeaky and coarse. A respiratory technician threaded a tube the size of thick spaghetti through her mouth and into her chest. Into the tube she placed the milky fluid that would coat the baby's lungs. She connected her to a small portable ventilator that delivered oxygen at a constant pressure, and tapped her finger over a hole in the tube to pace the breaths. The baby's chest heaved mechanically.

She weighed 570 grams—1 pound, 4 ounces. She was 11.4 inches long —the length of a Barbie doll.

I saw Gwen roll the incubator past. Inside was a raw dark creature, a blur in a too-big hat. My husband looked at me and looked at the baby.

"Go with her," I said. "Please go."

A baby at 23 weeks' gestation has just begun to hear, but can't yet see. It may recognize its mother's voice. It has a dawning awareness of whether it is right side up or upside down. The surface of its brain is smooth, just beginning to develop the hills and valleys that become wrinkles and folds. It responds to pain, but has no capacity for memory or for complex thought. Its lungs look like scrawny saplings compared to the full, bushy trees of normal lungs. Its bones are soft. It swallows. Its hair and eyelashes are just starting to grow and its fingernails and fingerprints are just forming. Its body is covered with a soft protective down. It is recognizably human, but barely.

I was still in recovery when Tom returned from the NICU, crying.

"She's so perfect," he said. His voice was a squeak. "She's so beautiful."

I just stared at him. My sweet, emotional husband, in the grip of something terrifying and overwhelming. He'd been to a place I couldn't fathom.

"That's my baby girl up there," he kept saying. "That's my daughter."

I used to imagine what I would say to her when I first saw her. She'd be wrapped in a blanket and wearing a hat, and she'd feel solid in my arms, like a puppy. She might open one eye and peek up at me, perplexed but curious. She would know my voice and my smell, know I was her mother, and because she knew that, she would not be afraid. I'd be hit with a force that would unmake me and remake me, right there.

Instead I waited in recovery while she fought for her life somewhere beyond my reach. After seven hours Tom took me up to the NICU in a wheelchair, still in my cotton surgical gown, lugging an IV pole.

Tom pushed my wheelchair up to the deep sink so I could scrub my hands. There were posted instructions and a disposable scrub brush and I felt determined to do it properly, for the full 30 seconds, in the hottest possible water, as if precise compliance with the rules might tip the odds.

I saw her plastic box halfway across the room. I didn't see anything else, just this tunnel of space and time and of everything changing that marked the distance between us. Here I was one person and there I would become someone else. The soap was hard to rinse, and I let the water run for a long time.

Tom wheeled me to her portholed plastic box. The nurse introduced herself as Gwen, but I barely heard her. There, through the clear plastic, was my daughter. She was red and angular, angry like a fresh wound. She had a black eye and bruises on her body. Tubes snaked out of her mouth, her belly button, her hand. Wires moored her to monitors. Tape obscured her face. Her chin was long and narrow, her mouth agape because of the tubes. Dried blood crusted the corner of her mouth and the top of her diaper. The diaper was smaller than a playing card, and it swallowed her. She had no body fat, so she resembled a shrunken old man, missing his teeth. Her skin was nearly translucent, and through her chest I could see her flickering heart.

She kicked and jerked. She stretched her arms wide, palms open, as if in welcome or surrender.

I recognized her. I knew the shape of her head and the curve of her butt. I knew the strength of her kick. I knew how she had fit inside me, and felt an acute sensation that she had been cut out, and of how wrong that was.

I had crazy thoughts. Should we prepare a birth announcement? What would we name her? If she died, would we get a birth certificate? Would there be a funeral? Would we get a box of ashes, and if so, what size box? Was she aware of us? Did she recognize me like I recognized her? Was she afraid? Did she wonder where I had gone? If she ever got out of this box, would she know I was her mother?

She was alien and familiar. She was terrifying and beautiful. She was complete and interrupted. I felt the icy hush that comes with looking at a secret you are not meant to see. I was peeking into God's pocket.

"You can touch her," Gwen said.

I reached in through the porthole. I saw how white and swollen my hand was. I let it hover over her for a second, then pulled away, as if from a fire. Finally I placed the tip of my pinky into her tiny palm.

She grabbed on.

THE ZERO ZONE

We were cast into a neverland of sick babies, where every moment is a fight for existence.

PART TWO

Bent double, I shuffled down a winding corridor, trying to find my baby.

Somewhere in this place my new daughter lay alone in a neonatal intensive care unit, struggling to breathe. I could feel the stabbing incision where they had cut her out of me two days before. That's how it felt—like there had been an assault, perhaps in an alley with a dull spoon. The doctors had been kind and correct, and they'd had no choice. But they might as well have taken my liver, or my heart.

The curving pastel hallways felt infinite. I'd visited her—a raw and tiny thing, born four months premature—but could not remember how to get back there, and I wasn't supposed to go alone.

I clutched a syringe containing a trace amount of milk. Since her birth, I'd spent nearly every hour in a hospital bed attached to an electric pump, a frustrating and painful exercise that only magnified the absurdity of the situation. My body did not seem to know what to do. It was April 2011 and the baby wasn't due until August, yet here she was. Everything was out of synch.

I had wrung out a few drops and collected them in this syringe, like you'd use to feed an orphaned squirrel. It was a pathetic amount, but the nurses insisted the baby needed every drop. Her underdeveloped gut was vulnerable to infection and rupture, calamities that killed many babies her size. My milk could coat her stomach lining with protective antibodies. The pressure to produce the stuff was immense. If one more nurse called it "liquid gold," I was going to spit.

The odds said she would die. I wondered how much time we had. I couldn't hold her or feed her. She couldn't see me. I didn't know if she was aware of me at all. I could do nothing to tip the odds, or even to assert myself as her mother, except deliver this milk.

My insides screamed. Vicodin had been prescribed, but I had skipped the dose because I wanted to keep drugs out of the milk. I came to the long window of what I thought of as the Fat Baby Nursery. This was the place for healthy newborns—goliaths who wailed petty complaints with robust lungs. "What's your problem, fatty?" I said to one. No 9-pounder had any right to complain.

I took a staff elevator up three floors. At a pair of locked double doors I picked up a phone. "I'm here to visit my daughter," I said. Daughter. The word was so unfamiliar it caught in my throat.

Inside a nurse guided me to her and took the milk from my hand.

"Is it enough?" I asked.

It was 1 mL, a thimbleful, but just enough for a baby so small. The nurse attached it to the tube snaking into the baby's mouth and down to her belly.

It was gone in a second.

I always knew I'd have a daughter. I pictured her with a puppy in her lap and dirt under her nails. She'd make me laugh and she'd refuse to wear shoes. I had carried and shaped the idea of her as long as I could remember.

When I started dating Tom French, I watched him load the dishwasher with his two boys—they did a sloppy job but they sang the whole time—and I knew he should be her dad. He was nearing 50 and wary of starting over. Convincing him took a breakup now referred to in our house as the Dark Era. I never questioned why I wanted a daughter so much. She was a real person to me. I would will her into existence.

Conceiving her took four years of fertility treatments—pills and vials, needles in my arms, needles in my stomach, needles in my butt, surgeries and so many wands and gloves shoved into my nether regions that it stopped seeming strange. After three failed in-vitro fertilizations, it took an egg donor, too. The donor was a friend of mine. A better friend, it turned out, than I even knew. We worked out the details over pomegranate margaritas, and when the test came back positive, she was the first person I called.

I didn't mourn the broken limb on my family tree. I was excited about the genes I'd chosen for my daughter, on both sides. I imagined that someday she'd thank me for the blue eyes and dark hair she was bound to inherit. She didn't have my DNA, but when she squirmed inside my belly, I knew she was mine.

Then she was snatched away at birth, and the umbilical cord connecting us was cut and replaced with lines connecting her to machines.

Tom and I had stretched the limits of science once already, to create her. To keep her, we'd have to do it again. The doctors said we could end up with a live baby, a dead baby, or a wrecked baby. Before we'd know, we would explore the wonder and peril of man's ability to manipulate nature, and we'd surrender to the understanding that we control so little.

Would my baby and I find our way back to each other? Was I really a mother now? Was mother a noun or a verb, and what did it mean, in this strange place?

The neonatal intensive care unit at All Children's Hospital was a world out of science fiction. Before, there had been only my baby in my body. Now we found ourselves in a multimillion-dollar artificial womb. The work of my balking uterus was replicated by an army of specialists in a facility that looked like an alien hive.

There were rows of incubators covered with quilts to shut out light and sound. I couldn't see or approach the babies inside. I expected to hear crying, but babies didn't cry here. Their faces contorted in protest, but the tubes in their throats stopped the sound. The machines beeped and alarmed. The room swarmed with people in scrubs. Here and there sat bleary parents in various stages of boredom and shock. I did not know my place in this new world.

The NICU was a technological triumph. Science had made life possible at earlier and earlier stages of development, but inside those possibilities, terrible bargains were made. Science, ambition, compassion and common sense collided here, every day.

Another parent once called it the Zero Zone, and when I heard that, my mind flooded with context and understanding. It was a place that existed outside of time, apart from everything I used to know and from the person I used to be. It was as if I'd been jerked out of my own shoes, out of the life I recognized. Every second was an improbable gift and an agonizing eternity. Would my baby die today? Would she die before lunch? If I left for an hour, would she die while I was gone? There was no future, no past. There was only a desperate struggle to maintain.

The Zero Zone. The idea became hypnotic, took on multiple interpretations. Our baby was born at a unique window of time, at 23 weeks and six days' gestation. She was a thwarted miscarriage, not yet fully her own person with her own standing. Because the questions were so unanswerable, the decision to put her on life support and allow her a chance to live had belonged to Tom and me, not the doctors and not the state.

This place was a frontier. Between life and death, certainly, but also between right and wrong, and between who we used to be and who we were becoming.

There were 97 beds taking up an entire floor of All Children's Hospital. Ninety babies were admitted that April. About a quarter were drug babies —mostly oxycodone—and the rest were genetic disorders, birth defects and preemies. We became aware of babies with missing limbs, holes in their spines, shunts in their brains. Two babies were born that month at the edge of viability. I never saw the other one.

Parents were oddly scarce. The chairs by many of the incubators stayed empty. All Children's took babies from as far away as the Caribbean. Some parents couldn't make the trip. Some were in prison or rehab. And some, faced with the fragility and complexity of life here, simply fled. Babies lingered alone until they were discharged to foster care. Volunteers held and fed them. Nurses rocked them while they did their charts.

We saw a mom who could not have been older than 18, sitting alone in a wheelchair, holding her gown closed in the back with her hand. I could see her baby's intestines piled in a bag atop his stomach. I desperately wanted to take her out for a milk shake. But we never spoke.

We saw a couple no older than 16, surrounded by family and balloons. The boy looked barely old enough to shave. We expected him to disappear, but he came back day after day in his white undershirt and too-big shorts. "Do you have any questions?" the doctors would ask. They'd just shake their heads.

One afternoon we watched someone pull a privacy screen around a family gathered at one of the incubators, and our nurse ushered us out. When we returned, the family was gone, and inside the incubator, underneath the blankets, was a shape, not moving. The blankets were perfectly tucked and smoothed. On the floor were an empty alcohol packet and two crumpled tissues. The dead baby stayed there for hours. The nurses did not speak of these things, did not look in the direction of the lump under the blanket, but their mouths grew tight. In this place, death was not theoretical.

I would think about the dead baby every day. I would imagine when that day would come for me. The nurses would sit me down in the blue vinyl recliner. They would turn to the baby and unhook the tubes and wires, one by one. They'd gently lift my daughter out of the incubator, wrap her in a blanket, and lay her in my arms. She'd be sedated, so she wouldn't struggle, but she'd gasp. My husband would want to hold her, but I'd cling to her as long as I could. I would be a mother for a moment. I would try to say something a dying baby would need her mother to say. "You are not alone. I love you more than the world." I would memorize her face. I would be terrified of forgetting. We would pass her back and forth until she grew cold and mottled and dark. It would take longer than you'd think. The stethoscope would leave an imprint on her chest.

We would walk away not knowing who we were.

Nurse practitioner Diane Loisel stopped by Bed 692, where we sat frozen and numb. She lifted the quilt and peered at the day-old baby inside.

We recognized her as the person who'd led us to the decision not to let our baby die. I felt solid ground for the first time in days.

Our baby was a tiny thing, Diane said, but wiggly. That was a decent sign. Diane opened a porthole and used a stethoscope the size of a quarter to listen to the baby's lungs. They sounded clear on both sides. She looked at the ventilator settings. The baby was receiving 21 percent oxygen—the same amount as in the air around us. Excellent.

Diane listened to her gut as she moved from baby to baby. Something about this baby encouraged her. The first week, though, was often called the honeymoon period. She warned us that things could turn in a flash.

We reminded her that we did not want to torture our baby with futile treatment.

Diane nodded. "She looks good for now," she said.

"But you'll let me know when to freak out, right?" I said.

"I will tell you when to freak out."

I'd slept maybe five hours in the first five days. I had vomit in my hair. The capillaries under my eyes were busted from crying. I wasn't allowed to drive. As if that wasn't enough, the people in charge of birth certificates were hounding me at all hours. They wanted a name and they by-God wanted it now. They left a baby name book in my hospital room. They stalked me wielding blank forms.

Tom and I had been in such collision over names we'd agreed to table the question until the third trimester. We finally stole a name a friend had given his daughter: Juniper. We called her Junebug.

Someone wrote her name on a card on the foot of her incubator with her birth weight: 570 grams. One pound 4 ounces. I've eaten burritos at Chipotle that were bigger than that.

She was so fragile that even the delicate handling after birth had left her bruised. All her fine details—hair, eyelids, fingernails—looked slightly blurry, like a partially developed Polaroid. Her head was smaller than a tennis ball. Her ears had no cartilage, so they crumpled. She had no nipples —they wouldn't form for a few more weeks. The ventilator made her belly heave with such force her chest dimpled under the ribs. Wires snaked from electrodes on her chest. A red sensor glowed on her foot. An IV ran into her hand. A wheeled pole next to her bed was stacked with three levels of pumps dosing out caffeine, antibiotics, pain medication and sedatives. A hanging bag contained liquid intravenous nutrition, precisely calibrated each day. She was so obscured by tape and technology that I struggled to imagine her naked face.

The biggest fear was intraventricular hemorrhage: bleeding in the brain. Vessels could burst from the stress of delivery or a surge in blood pressure. Blood could clot, causing pressure to build. Brain tissue could die, destroying the capacity for movement, language, learning. A bad enough brain bleed would mean taking her off life support.

Her intestines were vulnerable to infection and rupture. In times of stress, the body diverts blood to the brain and heart first, the gut last. A lack of circulation could make her belly distend and turn black. Her intestines could die, poisoning her from the inside.

The ventilator kept her alive, but the pressure stretched her tiny air sacs, scarring her lungs. A surge in pressure—from aggressive resuscitation, for example—could burst the air sacs. Too much pressure in the blood vessels could fill the lungs with blood, drowning her.

Antibiotics to ward off infection could shut down the kidneys. Oxygen to keep her alive could make her blind. Narcotics to keep her comfortable could make her an addict.

Nurse Tracy Hullett warned us to keep our hopes in check.

"Never trust a preemie," she said.

I watched Nurse Tracy attach a tiny bow to Juniper's forehead using KY Jelly. I didn't know what to make of all the pumps and monitors, and I struggled to follow the medical babble, but I understood the meaning in that small gesture.

This is your daughter. Get to know her.

I used medical tape to attach a photo of Tom and me to her isolette, so when her eyes opened, she would know who her parents were. For the harder stuff, I was lost. How do you connect with a little girl who can't see or eat or cry? How do you parent a baby in a plastic box?

Tracy showed us how to tuck a thermometer under the baby's arm to take her temperature. It was shocking how strong she was and how hard she fought, swatting and kicking blindly with her chicken limbs. Tracy showed us how to change the tiny diaper, which she trimmed with scissors so it fit just right. We had to hold it with just our fingertips, being careful to avoid the wires, and tuck a cotton ball inside to collect the pee.

She measured Juniper's belly and head to check for swelling that would indicate a bleed or a break. When she changed the leads on the baby's chest, she touched the sticky side with her fingers to weaken the glue so it wouldn't pull off skin. On good days, she let us lift the baby while she changed the blankets. She fit easily in our hands, but her arms and legs would flail, pulled by the weight of the IVs, and we'd have to be careful not to dislodge the ventilator tube in her throat. Tracy showed us how to touch the baby. Her skin was so new and the nerves so close to the surface that stroking rankled her. She liked firm, steady pressure that made her feel secure, like in the womb. We'd cup one hand around her head and the other around her feet. We could feel the huge soft spots throbbing in her unfused skull.

Tracy would gently turn her each time she tucked her in, so the baby's soft head wouldn't flatten on the sides. It was an effect common in preemies that the nurses called "toaster head." Once I learned about toaster heads I saw them everywhere. In the elevator. In the grocery. Preemie! I'd think, proud of my new diagnostic abilities. I wanted my baby to be brilliant and have a nice round head like Charlie Brown, but mostly I wanted her to live. If she ended up with a head like a kitchen appliance, well, kids look so great in hats.

I shared every one of my rambling, crazed thoughts with Tracy, and she didn't appear to judge me.

Tracy moved quietly, in the background, and was hard to read. While the other nurses wore scrubs featuring teddy bears or Disney characters, Tracy's had cats from outer space. She was meticulous, but had a gift for improvisation. She hemmed her pants with staples.

She was 48. She didn't have kids of her own and didn't want them. She joked that she lost interest in babies once they cut teeth. That was fine with me. I wanted her to save our baby's life, not teach her to water-ski. She had a soft spot for wounded things. She had a houseful of rescued cats. She came to remind me of a cat. She was stealthy.

Tracy was undaunted by doctors. When one ordered a barrage of blood tests, she calmly picked up a phone to remind him that the baby had a little more than an ounce of blood in her whole body. "This baby doesn't have that much blood to give," Tracy said. "You're going to have to decide which tests you want the most."

We'd been told that one important advantage we could give our baby was to convince a great nurse to take her on as a primary patient. I made Tom ask. I didn't think I could handle it if Tracy said no. I could see the conversation from across the room, and Tracy looked cornered. She was collected as always, but her step quickened when she walked away.

"She said she'd think about it," Tom said. "She's really busy."

The truth was, Tracy told me later, she did not want to get attached.

If she agreed, she'd spend every shift with us and Juniper, enduring all the terror in a much more personal way. She'd had many primaries over the years, and kept stacks of photos of them at home. She'd attended their birthday parties and pushed them on swings. She'd seen their high school graduations. She'd seen them grow up with blindness, cerebral palsy, wheelchairs and adult diapers. She'd attended their funerals, with their tiny open caskets.

One baby's parents lived far away, so Tracy had taken home the blankets and laundry herself and washed them with her scrubs. That baby lived eight months in the NICU and then died. Another was discharged to medical foster care and died the next day. The family of one baby who had died still sent a Christmas card every year.

Juniper was going to be a lot of work. Tracy was not at all sure she was going to survive.

She liked the baby's spunk, though. She'd chuckle when the tiny girl batted at her with her spindly arms.

"Listen, young lady," Tracy told her as we watched. "I have been wrestling preemies for a long time, and I am not afraid of you."

No one knew what kind of card to send. Were we celebrating or grieving? Even we didn't know.

"Congratulations!" people said, but that didn't seem quite right.

Friends and co-workers filled our freezer with Italian food from Mazzaro's. They held back the baby gifts they'd bought, not knowing if they would ever be used. Juniper had lots of visitors, but when they saw her they would step back and gasp. One family member was so unnerved he threw up.

Everyone, it seemed, knew somebody who knew somebody who was born at 1 pound and went on to have a remarkable life. My husband's co-worker's wife. A waitress' father. Without exception, it seemed, these babies were tucked into shoe boxes and kept warm by the oven.

"When can you take her home?" people asked, and it always stung.

Ours wasn't the world's smallest baby. Babies weighing just over 9 ounces have survived, and ours weighed more than twice that. But gestational age, not birth weight, is the key predictor of how a baby will do. Our baby was born so early some hospitals would have refused to save her. If she had come one week earlier, All Children's would have declined to try. In less developed countries, resuscitation would have been impossible. In the Netherlands, it would have been all but forbidden.

When she was 4 days old, I was discharged. Tom pushed me out in a wheelchair, no baby in my arms, no balloons. I cried on the curb.

"It's a miracle," people would say. I'd thank them and grind my teeth and think, Ask me in a year if it's a miracle.

At home on the fifth day, I felt uneasy in a way I couldn't explain. I asked Tom to call the NICU, because I was afraid to dial the phone myself. Jackie, the nurse that day, said Juniper was fine. She was wearing a pink hat and resting on a pink blanket. The feeling didn't go away. I asked Tom to call again that afternoon. She was still fine.

That evening a young nurse named Whitney Hoertz started her shift at 6. She looked at the monitors and the chart. All good. She looked at the results of that afternoon's chest X-ray. All good. She looked at the baby.

Juniper's belly looked a little dark, maybe, but it could be hard to tell in the light. Whitney got out a measuring tape and wrapped it under and around her. Her belly measured 18 cm—it had grown by 1.5 cm since that morning. She called a doctor, who called for an X-ray.

We were arriving at the hospital to see Juniper when we got the call. Her intestine had ruptured. Air and stool were spilling and collecting in her abdomen, flooding it with bacteria. The doctors suspected a terrifying and often fatal condition called necrotizing enterocolitis. It was the very problem I'd hoped to inoculate her against by pumping so much milk.

Her body hadn't deteriorated to the point that the monitors would register any trouble. Whitney's hunch had been the only warning.

We rushed upstairs to find a gathering at her bedside. The lid was off the incubator, and she lay there, distended and subdued. We each held her hands in our fingertips for a second. Then surgeons inserted a drain, like a soft drinking straw, to wick away the gunk in her belly. All we could do was wait to see if she healed, or if infection took her down, or if her intestines died off. It was a good thing she'd been getting breast milk, they said. Maybe it would help.

We struggled to find the right thing to say to the 28-year-old who had seen what the monitors could not.

"Whitney," Tom said. "Whitney ..."

"I know," she said. "I don't know what would've happened either."

Tracy was off that day, but Whitney was a reminder that an army of people watched over our baby—nurses, nurse practitioners, neonatologists, respiratory technicians, lactation consultants, specialists of all kinds. The hospital cleaning lady prayed for Juniper while she swept.

We stayed there all that night.

"I just don't want her to be alone," Tom said.

We watched the numbers flash on the monitor—the green number for the heart rate. The white number for her breathing. The blue number for the oxygen saturation in her blood. Those numbers were mesmerizing. The monitor alarmed whenever something got out of whack—about every 15 minutes. I stared at it, not sleeping, as the floor grew quiet and the windows grew dark.

Tom, fighting tears, opened a book and rested it on the lid of the incubator and began to read. It was an act of faith, I suppose, that he did not choose *Goodnight Moon* or *Go, Dog, Go!* He started with Chapter One of book one of the Harry Potter series, a series that totaled more than 4,000 pages. I knew he intended to read the entire thing, all seven books, even if it took him seven years.

"Chapter One," he began. "The Boy Who Lived."

The book tells the story of a baby who survived an attack by the most powerful evil in the world. He survived because his mother stood by his crib and protected him with her life.

Before dawn. Tom slumped in the chair next to me. A technician rolled a portable ultrasound machine to Juniper's bedside. He raised the lid and delicately cradled her head in one hand. With the other hand he placed the ultrasound wand against the wide, pulsing fontanelle. My heart hit my throat and I nudged Tom awake.

This was the test that would show us whether she had suffered bleeding in her brain. I'd been too upset about her belly to remember that it was scheduled for today, her sixth day of life. If it showed a massive bleed, the prognosis could mean severe disabilities. That, combined with the life-threatening rupture in her belly, would mean we would take her off life support, because how much insult can a 1-pound baby take?

I tried to divine some meaning from the image on the monitor. I saw the gray expanse of her brain and, inside it, two pools of black. I knew from the many ultrasounds during my pregnancy that black meant fluid. They looked like oil spills.

Blood? The technician, I knew, would tell us nothing.

I whispered to Tom, "Is fluid black?"

"I don't know, sweetie," he said, taking in the machine, the tech, the monitor. "Let's not jump to conclusions."

There's a saying in neonatology—"waiting to declare." Doctors will say that they stabilize the babies at birth and then wait for them to declare themselves—their intentions and their will—either by improving or deteriorating.

We were done with the honeymoon period now. We were waiting for Juniper to declare.

Tom and I were still cramped and bleary in the chairs next to the incubator when we saw a small, slow-moving battalion rolling through the unit. Morning rounds.

At the center of the group, Dr. Fauzia Shakeel wore a look like a battle commander.

She knew some of the nurses called her Terror Doc, and she was okay with that, because what did that matter to a sick baby? Rounds was the one chance she had to evaluate each baby and make critical decisions for the sickest ones. She wouldn't tolerate anyone showing up unprepared.

Diane, the nurse practitioner, read from the chart. "This is Juniper French, day of life six, she weighs 600 grams, up 40 from yesterday." She bristled under Dr. Shakeel's firm command. Even I sat up straighter in my chair.

Dr. Shakeel already knew what was in the chart. When she had a critical baby, she read it herself ahead of time.

Worsening blood gases ... metabolic acidosis ... penrose draining blood-tinged fluid...

Dr. Shakeel glanced at us, sitting so tense in our chairs. I chewed maniacally on a cuticle.

The computer showed a new report from radiology that morning. An ultrasound of the brain. It showed the two perfectly normal brain cavities that look like oil spills in the picture.

Dr. Shakeel looked up from the monitor, softened and smiled.

"Her head is fine," she said.

She continued to not die.

Some nights, she needed 90 percent oxygen to keep going. If the baby gets to 100 percent and keeps deteriorating, there's not much more they can do. The ventilator was damaging her lungs, so they put her on a gentler oscillating machine that made her whole body vibrate. There was no rhythmic in-and-out, no visual cue that she was a living, breathing person. Just a bizarre, full-body shudder.

Her black eye faded into a dark crescent. Her eyelashes grew longer. Her skin became lighter and more opaque.

No one discussed it, and we weren't aware of it until much later, but when the brain scan came back clean we'd crossed a threshold. She still faced death or an array of handicaps. But the test suggested her brain could be okay. She could someday laugh, sing, call me Mom.

We began to feel we could communicate with her, a little. We spoke to her nonstop, and she never made a sound, though sometimes we could tell she was crying. We learned that very early babies are animal-like in how they perceive the energy in a room. The monitor would alarm when she was bothered by something—a loud voice or a tense conversation.

"If you have to cry," one of the nurses told me, "try not to do it by the isolette."

The measure of the oxygen saturation in her blood—the blue number on the monitor—was an easy, constant register of her overall state. I related it to the grading scale in college. If I saw 90s, she got an A. But anything below 85 was cause for intervention.

We knew she could crash any time. Sometimes Tracy turned the monitor around so I couldn't see it.

Tom finished Chapter Two of Harry Potter and then Chapter Three. I would listen to him read and stare at the saturation number. Juniper seemed to enjoy the book. 97 ... 98 ... But when he would act out the gruff voice of Hagrid the half-giant, her oxygen saturation would plummet and the alarms would sound. 78! 76! 74!!

I swatted Tom on the shoulder. "You're scaring the baby," I said. "Stop doing Hagrid."

"No way," Tom said. He kept reading.

Ding! Ding! Ding!

Thereafter, Tom read every paragraph in a sweet, singsong voice. The alarm stayed quiet. In this way we learned what music she liked—Bruce Springsteen's "Waitin' on a Sunny Day" became our theme song. She had never seen the sun.

We developed a routine. Tom, who had raised two fine boys, always told me that being a good parent starts with showing up. Every morning he left the house in the dark. He never complained, he simply sat beside our baby as the sun rose.

I stayed home and strapped on the breast pump, grumbling and spilling milk on myself in the dark. The machine's rhythmic croaking mocked and insulted me. You're pathetic, it said. You're pathetic. You're pathetic.

I was biologically unfit for motherhood. I had failed to conceive her, failed to carry her, and now struggled to make enough milk to feed her. If I were a farm animal, I'd be culled from the herd.

Tom learned the name of every person on the floor. He baked 12 dozen chocolate chip cookies. I would have resented his campaign for Father of the Year if I hadn't been so grateful for it.

"I thought if they got to know us, and got to know our baby, maybe they'd pay closer attention," he told me. Then his voice dropped to a whisper. "Maybe if something happened, they'd run a little faster."

Tracy was around more and more. She never announced it, but we got the idea that she'd decided to be our primary nurse after all.

The hospital wasn't so much a place we visited as a place we existed. It was our baby's home, so it became ours too. All of our flaws and insecurities were on display. I wore my pajamas there every day for weeks.

When I cried, though, I did it in the car.

"Do you want to hold her today?"

She was 2 weeks old. We had family arriving from out of town that day. Our nurse was one we hadn't met before. I wondered if she knew what she was doing, or had missed the memo about how sick our baby was. I glanced around for doctors, or security personnel, who might try to stop her.

Then I just settled into the blue vinyl recliner and watched as a physical therapist spent half an hour massaging and calming my baby to prepare her for the 3-foot journey to my chest.

The therapist explained what should have been obvious. Babies need their moms. In the early days of neonatology, parents didn't get to hold their sick babies. Now, doctors knew that even the most critical held their body temperature better, breathed better, digested food better and generally fared better if they spent time skin to skin with their parents.

All Children's had designed this NICU to put families at the center, with round-the-clock visitation and an elaborate support system for breast-feeding.

Therapists like Ana Maria Jara helped the smallest babies navigate the divide between the safe dark nest of the womb and the bright stark world of the hospital. We watched her massage Juniper with the tip of her finger. Juniper's face contorted into a silent cry, then relaxed. She melted into Ana Maria's hands.

"They don't listen to your words," Ana Maria explained. "They listen to your feelings." We called her the Preemie Whisperer.

Ana Maria showed us how to tuck Juniper's knees under her and move her hands to her face. She gathered all the tubes and wires so nothing would tug at the baby when she was moved. She spoke softly to her in English and in Spanish.

"Que pasa, la nina?"

Tom recorded it all on the iPhone. I just grinned, crazily. I didn't wonder why they were letting me hold her so soon. Much later I'd ask about it and learn what I would have seen if I hadn't been so deep in denial. The nurse, the physical therapist and Dr. Shakeel had agreed that the baby was having a rare good day, and that this might be my only chance to hold her while she was still alive.

When all was ready, Ana Maria lifted Juniper. She moved her slowly, on a straight plane, careful not to jostle the ventilator tube even a few millimeters, because doing so could dislodge it. Finally she placed her on my chest and tucked her inside my shirt. Her feet kicked my ribs, and her head rested right under my chin. I put my hand on her back and watched the monitor as she began to breathe easier and easier. 97 ... 98 ... 99.

Just as she was settled, Tom's brother and sister arrived from the airport. Everyone gathered around wide-eyed, taking in how tiny she was, how wrinkled and dark, and how safe she looked. I don't know if she felt it, but she was part of a family then. They greeted her not as a mishap or as a possibility, but wholeheartedly, as one of a tribe.

Ana Maria told me to breathe deeply and calmly and the baby would copy me and we would fall into a rhythm together. I tried to project strength and comfort with every breath. I don't know if Juniper picked up on all that, or if she even knew where she was. But I like to believe she did.

She was so bony and so light. Like a baby bird, I thought. I breathed for both of us.

2:17 a.m. The phone jangled us awake.

ALL CHILDREN'S NICU

Tom answered. I could hear Dr. Aaron Germain's ultra-calm voice on the other end of the line.

"How far away do you live?" he said.

No one used the word, but she was dying.

Her intestine had ruptured a second time. The drains weren't working. She was breathing pure oxygen and it still wasn't enough. If she survived, so much oxygen could make her blind. She was swelling and retaining fluid, so they put in a catheter. Her blood pressure was faltering, so they pumped up her dopamine. Her organs weren't getting enough blood. Soon they would start to shut down.

Dr. Shakeel took over that morning. She told us that she had talked to the surgeon, who insisted she did not want to operate on a baby so small. The trip to the operating room could kill her, and they couldn't patch her intestine at the bedside. Once the surgeon cut her open, her skin was so papery she might not be able to get her closed.

Dr. Shakeel knew the surgery was a huge risk and a last resort, but what other option was there? Juniper was dying anyway. Later the doctor told me that she had debated it in her head for an hour. I've adjusted the vent. I've bumped up the drips. What else can I do?

These kinds of decisions were part of the job. She learned all she could, made the best decision she could, and then she never second-guessed herself. Her Muslim faith told her that God was in control. She let him guide her.

She knew numbers never told the whole story, and so, torn about what to do, she looked at the baby.

Juniper's eyes were just starting to open after being fused shut for so long. Now she opened them wide and looked right at her.

The doctor saw a baby who was almost a month old and not yet 2 pounds, whose body was shutting down, who was sedated and groggy and in so much pain, but was fighting to engage with the world. Her eyes were opening and closing. Opening and closing. Dr. Shakeel felt her saying, I'm here. I'm here.

Juniper French was declaring herself.

She was going to surgery. I held her hand. She was looking at me. Right at me, in a way she never had before. Her eyes were dark pools, taking in everything. Taking in my face, and my voice.

"It won't always be like this, baby.

"There are some things you need to know about. Like ice cream. You won't believe the chocolate milk shake at Coney Island. And at home there's a goofy dog named Muppet who will lick you too much, and her breath stinks but you can tell her all your secrets and she'll never share. You have your own room, with a big orange rug with a monkey on it. We'll take you to a Springsteen concert, if he can keep going long enough, and you can hear "Waitin' on a Sunny Day" and watch him slide across the stage. We'll take you to Fort De Soto and you can mush your toes in the sand. Someday you'll ride a horse bareback in the sun, and you'll go so fast your eyes will water. You'll dance in your jammies. You'll hold my hand and I'll take you to school, and when the bell rings, I'll be waiting for you."

They wheeled her away.

Dr. Beth Walford saw only the rectangle of dark flesh peeking through the surgical drape. The baby, smaller than a footlong sub, was shrouded in blue sheets. It was easier that way. A surgeon needed to focus.

She did not want to be in this position. Surgeons had a saying: "Never operate on a patient on the day of their death." If a kid was that sick, you probably weren't going to help. And if she died, it would be your failure too.

"Knife," she said. Out went her gloved hand, for the scalpel.

The X-ray showed air in the abdomen, which meant there was a hole somewhere in the intestine. She would have to find it. She'd rinse and clean the intestines, then cut out the holes and dead spots. She'd reroute part of the intestine so it emptied out the baby's side. That would give her lower intestines a rest. When the baby was bigger she'd put it all back together. She held the scalpel like an X-Acto knife and sliced horizontally, just above the belly button.

Cutting through the skin was easy. Eighties music was playing over the satellite radio. She peeled back the peritoneal wall, but what she saw made her freeze. In her head, the room got quiet. She couldn't hear the music anymore.

Everything inside was red and inflamed. The intestines were matted together, stuck to the peritoneal wall like old spaghetti would stick to a Tupperware lid. Dr. Walford picked up a pair of forceps and touched the tissue. It started to bleed. She was creating new holes, making things worse.

She became a surgeon because she wanted to fix people. But she couldn't fix this.

There are worse things than watching your baby die, I told myself.

Forgetting your baby in the back seat of a car on a hot day. That would be worse. But that happens to good people, all the time. Pulling a 2-year-old out of a swimming pool would be worse. Losing a child at any age greater than hers would be worse, because every day makes letting go so much harder. But these impossible goodbyes were happening right now, in this building. They happened here every day. They had been happening long before I had reason to pay attention.

My mind played a game as I walked the hospital's halls. I saw cute kids in the elevator or the cafeteria, and I tried to guess what was secretly wrong with them. I wondered if I would trade my problems for theirs. Big-eyed Hispanic kid in the lobby? Blood disease. Cute black kid in the parking garage? Heart trouble. Baby in the stroller in a full-body cast? Brittle bones.

I knew I would not trade. Even if she died, trying to save her had been the right decision. We'd gotten to know her. We'd let her hear our voice, and hear music, and feel our hands on her. Some of the greatest moments of my life had been tucked inside this misery. Memorizing her face. Holding her hand. Feeling her warm and weightless form on my chest. Reading her a story. Writing "mom" on a consent form. Every act, no matter how mundane, affirmed that this child belonged to me. If those moments were not so precious, there would be no terror, no cruelty, in seeing them snatched away.

"She's my daughter," Tom said. "I wouldn't change any of it."

The prayer book in the hospital chapel told the story. Every day, prayers were launched into the universe, to God, to Jehovah, and to Senor Jesucristo y mi Virgen Maria Guadalupe. Love and faith and grief bled through every page.

I am really scared. All I do is pray.

She doesn't know it, but she is my world.

Well, God. I've been praying every day, but sometimes the answer is not what we want. I trust you. Take care of her.

Thank you Lord for one more day.

I thought about all the people who'd told us they were praying for our baby. Churches we'd never set foot in. Our friend's mother had her Catholic church praying in New York. Some of Tom's friends had gotten word to a mosque in India, where 700 people gathered just to pray for Juniper. Some spiritual types in Atlanta were meditating on it. My friend Lucia had an altar set up on her fireplace mantel, with candles burning. The people at Preacher's Barbecue held hands and prayed for Juniper before they handed us our ribs. I began to think of all this prayer as a big cloud over us, sheltering us.

I didn't know it, but somewhere in the cloud of prayer rising up out of that hospital was the voice of Dr. Shakeel.

That afternoon, as we waited for word from the surgeon, Dr. Shakeel retreated to a small room near the NICU and kneeled on her prayer rug. She had exhausted her expertise, pushed technology to its limit. Now she surrendered.

She faced east toward Mecca. She spoke to the one who creates life and brings death, the one with the power to heal. She told God he was in control. She asked for his help. She touched her forehead to the ground.

* * *

BABY'S BREATH

As our daughter lay in the NICU, we wondered: What does a miracle look like?

PART THREE

The surgeon sewed our baby shut. The neonatologist rose from her prayer rug. Then a nurse returned our tiny daughter to the quiet of her incubator, and we made our bargains with God.

The surgeon wouldn't say it, but she was certain our baby would be dead by morning.

That night, Dr. Fauzia Shakeel had trouble sleeping and logged into the All Children's Hospital network to check on Juniper. Nurse Tracy Hullett picked up an overtime shift so that if our daughter died, she'd know she'd done all she could. Tom and I arrived at the hospital early, walked past the kids climbing the pelican sculpture, past the painted hot air balloons. I wondered if, by the time we left that night, I'd no longer be a mom.

Dr. Shakeel stopped by Juniper's incubator that afternoon, where I sat curled, pale and fetal, in the chair.

"Babies are very, very resilient," she said. I had my chin on my hand and was rocking like a mental patient. Dr. Shakeel wrapped her arm around me.

"Where there's life," she told me, "there's hope."

Juniper didn't die that day and she didn't die the next. She didn't die all that week. I was terrified that she'd die on Mother's Day, but she didn't.

Maybe the simple act of cutting her open had relieved pressure in her abdomen, allowing her kidneys and lungs to function. Maybe one of the four soda-straw-sized drains the surgeon had inserted in desperation had made a difference.

"She's being a smart girl," Nurse Tracy told us. "Enjoy the moment."

She didn't die, but in a way she disappeared. She bloated until she became unrecognizable. Her head grew misshapen, waterlogged. She couldn't move. She couldn't open her eyes. She was awful to look at. I didn't tell anyone this, but I'd delivered a stillborn puppy once who looked like her. The sight of it had scared me so much I'd wrapped it in a dish towel and stuffed it in a plastic bag. Now I had to find a way to reach my daughter, wherever she had gone.

Sitting stoop-shouldered on the swivel chair by her incubator, occupying the same few square feet of space that had been our continent for the past month, I tried to build a world for my baby out of pieces that didn't fit. I couldn't hold her, couldn't feed her, and I didn't even know the right songs. My husband, Tom, had raised two sons and knew all the words to all the songs in *Mary Poppins* and *The Wizard of Oz*. I sang Johnny Cash.

When I was just a baby

My mama told me son

Always be a good boy, don't ever play with guns

But I shot a man in Reno, just to watch him die

I dredged my brain. Old country songs, TV jingles I hadn't heard since I was 10, half-remembered hymns. Bits and pieces of my own childhood dislodged from my subconscious and surfaced at my sick baby's bedside.

I talked to her about everything. She never reacted. I was aware of the sound of my own voice, of its rhythms and tone. I watched the monitor, but the clues were not there. I talked to God, too, but I did that in my head. I asked that Juniper have just one good day. She had lived more than a month, and each day had been measured in needle sticks, isolation and pain. She'd been held only once. I didn't know if my touching her brought her comfort or aggravation. I thought if she had one good day she would want one more, and another and another. Without that, what did she have to live for? Why would she fight?

Eventually I ran out of words. I picked up Harry Potter and turned to the folded-over page where Tom had left off. I hoped that something in my voice, or in the cadence of the language, would comfort her.

Tom, like me, is a writer. Stories for him are a source of meaning. The stories we chose carried messages of love and faith and friendship, and the shared experience of generations.

"A story is a promise," he said. "It's a promise that the end is worth waiting for."

That's what I wanted for her—to know that life was worth the fight. I read to her about the great green room with the telephone and the red balloon. As parents and children have done for decades, we invented new endings. "Good night Dr. Shakeel. Good night IV pole. Good night ventilator."

I read all of *Winnie the Pooh* and *The House at Pooh Corner*, and cried when Piglet sidled up to Pooh and took his hand and said, "I just wanted to be sure of you."

Nurse practitioner Diane Loisel folded back the quilt covering our baby's incubator and opened the portholes.

"Oh, little girl," she said, "little girl, little girl."

It was mid-May, about a week and a half after the failed surgery to repair Juniper's intestines. Under the gauze on her stomach the incision was a jagged gray gash. The drains placed by the surgeon had come out and the holes had scabbed over, but we wouldn't know for a few weeks whether her intestines had healed. Probably there would be scarring and blockages, and in the worst case, whole dead sections.

Diane probed Juniper's brown, distended belly, checking for firmness that would indicate pressure inside. It was soft: That was good. She wiped the scab on the right side where one of the drains had been and saw strange green goop on her gauze. This was bizarre. She wiped again. More goop.

It was poop. Coming from a place where poop should not be.

"Little one, little one, little one," Diane said.

A horrifying breach had opened in our baby's plumbing. But Diane, as always, was outwardly calm. It could even be a good thing, she told us. Had the surgery been successful, the surgeon would have created an escape hatch just like this in order to give Juniper's lower intestines a rest. The surgery had essentially failed, but Juniper's body had rerouted itself. It was sending poop out the most convenient exit. They would attach a little bag to the hole under her ribs to catch the poop, and add it to the list of things to fix later.

Diane noticed that Juniper had grown. She was almost 2 pounds, but so much of that was fluid from the swelling it was hard to guess her real weight. Diane brushed back the baby's hair with her fingertips, so gently, and touched what she could of her face, between the tubing and all the tape.

Tom asked the question he had asked before. "Have we pushed her too far?"

It was impossible not to wonder if we were torturing our baby. I could not imagine another area in medicine where the ethical questions were as immediate as here in the neonatal intensive care unit. All around us were sick infants unable to voice an opinion about their care or their quality of life. In front of us was one who couldn't tell us how much pain was too much. Where does medical progress blur into hubris?

Diane shook her head. No, we hadn't yet pushed her too far. "Not even close. But I'll tell you if we reach that point."

She didn't tell us that some of her colleagues had wondered the same thing. Do the parents still want everything done?

It was unsettling to think about what all this care was costing. Those thoughts led to uncomfortable questions about what Juniper's life, or anyone's life, is worth.

A day or two after Juniper was born, we'd met with a financial specialist at All Children's Hospital. When we sat down at her desk, I was gripping Tom's hand and nearly hyperventilating. I knew that medical disasters like this cost people their homes, their careers, their retirements, their marriages. I was paralyzed by the fear that if Juniper lived, she'd come home to a ruin of the family that had created her.

"You can't think about that right now," the financial specialist said. Babies born this young almost always exceeded $1 million in medical expenses, and if they had private insurance, they frequently hit their plans' lifetime caps. Most ended up on Medicaid. I was halfway to a panic attack when she said, "Well, this is amazing news." She swiveled toward us in her chair. "It's only going to cost you $400."

Four hundred what?

That was the copay for our baby's hospitalization. Everything that happened to Juniper until she was discharged would be covered by Blue Cross Blue Shield. We had one of the best private insurance plans she'd seen in a long time. There would be plenty of expenses later, but all I heard from that point forward was blah blah blah blah.

I was relieved, but also stung by the guilt that comes with privilege and luck. My husband had changed jobs a year earlier and was commuting every week from St. Petersburg to Bloomington, Indiana, where he taught at Indiana University. Our health plan came with no deductible or lifetime cap.

Still, Juniper's situation raised broader questions that are impossible to consider when a newborn baby is gasping for breath. How does one long-shot baby justify so much expense, when so many people go without health care?

One day, a friend asked me a difficult question, trusting that I knew she meant no harm.

"Don't take this the wrong way," she said, "but wouldn't it be better to vaccinate a million kids in Africa?"

I was sure a lot of people wondered the same thing. Health care was not strictly a personal issue. One way or another, society shared the costs.

I could have argued with her for an hour. Who are we to know when an investment in a child's life will pay off? If we don't cut off care to the very old, why would we deny it to the newly born?

I wanted to know more, though. So I dug into the research.

Babies born earlier than 28 weeks' gestation require an average of about $200,000 in medical care by age 7, said Dr. Norman J. Waitzman, an economist at the University of Utah. Waitzman worked on a major study in 2006 that put the cost of preterm birth in the United States at more than $26 billion per year.

The statements that arrived almost daily from our insurance company told another part of the story. It appeared that the neonatologist cost about $1,900 a day. A month in the NICU—presumably room, board and nursing care—was billed at between $200,000 and $450,000. Then there were the costs for surgeries, lab work and specialists. All together, Juniper's care cost more than $6,000 a day. The statements would add up to $2.4 million, of which the hospital collected from the insurance company a negotiated rate of $1.2 million.

Waitzman said Juniper's bill sounded typical for a baby born at 23 weeks. But because so few babies are born that early, their bills, however staggering, barely register in the big picture.

A study by bioethicist John Lantos and colleagues showed that 90 cents of each dollar spent in the NICU goes toward the care of kids who survive. This is true even for the tiniest babies. By contrast, most of the dollars spent on the elderly go to patients who die without ever leaving the hospital. The NICU, Lantos argues, is a bargain compared with adult intensive care, because dollars spent there buy many more years of life.

Neonatal intensive care for the sickest babies has become the most expensive intervention in pediatrics, Lantos has written. Because

Medicaid and insurance companies are willing to pay, NICUs are profit centers for many hospitals. Preemies often require further treatment in other departments—cardiology, neurology, pulmonology—so the tiniest babies run up total lifetime medical bills about double their NICU costs.

So, would it be better to spend the money on a million kids in Africa?

Standing there with my friend, I didn't wade into the complexities. I just answered honestly and reflexively, with the perspective of a desperate new mom.

"Better for who?"

One night in May, Juniper opened a swollen eye and peeked out.

The swelling subsided, then came back. We watched helplessly as one system in her body after another faltered and recovered.

By June, when she was 2 months old, we were hugging Dr. Shakeel goodbye and greeting a new doctor, our third. They rotated every three weeks because the most critical cases were hard on them too. Everyone was coming and going except us. We had been moved to our own room, 670, with a sliding glass door with Juniper's name on it. Best of all, it had a cabinet where we could stash our baby blankets, mouthwash and smuggled granola bars.

Dr. Rajan Wadhawan was our new neonatologist. He was calm and assertive, quick to smile, like the Dog Whisperer on TV. He asked us to sit down with him to review Juniper's progress. It felt like our first parent-teacher conference. When a baby was very sick, the doctors and nurses would say it was not behaving. I'd had a bad baby for a long time.

We sat on swivel chairs as Dr. Raj, as everyone called him, methodically reviewed the obstacles Juniper faced, in order of urgency.

A blood clot had been discovered that morning in her heart. It was about 6 mm, which seems small, but her heart was the size of a chicken's. Relatively speaking, it was a boulder. Blood clots either dissolve or dislodge.

If this one broke loose, it would slalom through her vessels until it reached her lung or her brain and killed her.

Fluid was leaking from a breach in her lymphatic system and pooling in her chest, crowding her lungs. Tubes had been placed in each side of her chest to drain the fluid so she could breathe. Four to 8 ounces poured out every day. The tubes hurt, so we couldn't hold her. The condition, called chylothorax, was a puzzle, not a typical preemie thing at all. It meant she couldn't be fed the breast milk I was still torturing myself to produce, because the fats in the milk exacerbated the problem. They stashed my milk in a hospital freezer and fed her through an IV. In a day or so they'd start giving her a foul concoction through a tube, testing her healing intestines.

Next came the scarring in her lungs from the ventilator, her mind-of-their-own intestines and the constant threat of infection. She was getting too few calories, growing too slowly. Her bones were brittle and her liver was stressed.

Death remained a real possibility. But I still clung to an image of a little girl holding my hand on the way to kindergarten. I couldn't help it. The longer she held on, the more I wanted my daydreams back.

"Just one more question," I said. "Could she still be a normal kid?"

Dr. Raj rattled off some research, but in a field that changed so fast, it added up to maybe.

I held a sleeping baby in my arms.

It wasn't my baby. This was a baby from down the hall, Jack Cole, who'd been born with Down syndrome. We'd met his parents when they were still shaken by the news that he needed surgery to save his life. Their faces had been clouded with exhaustion and fear, but something else, too. Joy.

"We just can't wait to take him home and love him," his dad said.

When I told his mom, Danielle, that we couldn't hold Juniper, she'd plopped Jack in my arms, just like that. I looked at him, all soft cheeks and soft breath and soft hair.

They said it would not have mattered if they had known he had Down syndrome. I envied them for that.

Jack was beautiful, but in his extra chromosome I saw a parallel to our worst fears.

Doctors had told us Juniper would probably die or be disabled. We'd considered letting her die rather than face the odds. Why did we struggle so much when Jack's parents seemed so content?

Society seems fairly comfortable with Down babies. But in 1982, not so long ago, the parents of a Bloomington, Indiana, baby with Down syndrome declined an esophageal surgery that would have saved his life. The case got national attention, and surgeon general C. Everett Koop argued that it was child abuse to withhold treatment to a baby because of a mental handicap. The Baby Doe case forced doctors, hospitals, and parents to confront how they make decisions about withholding treatment in disabled newborns, and how they weigh quality of life.

Thirty years later, parents still struggled with a diagnosis of Down syndrome, and many aborted their babies after prenatal testing. But once a child was born with the condition, there was more of a consensus in the medical community to provide treatment. Kids with Down syndrome were in Target ads. There was even one on *Glee*.

There was no such consensus when it came to the earliest preemies like Juniper. Maybe the issues were still too new. Maybe it was easier to confront a well-defined disability like Down syndrome than a buffet of probabilities.

Looking at Jack, I knew that whatever became of Juniper, I'd love and defend her. But I wished for a little of the certainty and joy I saw in Jack's parents. I wished for a little of the clarity the doctors could offer them about his future. I hoped that whatever happened, I'd be as accepting of Juniper as they were of Jack.

I made a promise to myself, and to her, that I would be.

She sounded, at first, like a kitten.

On the 59th day, her breathing tube came out. For a quick second, I saw her unobstructed mouth and chin. I saw her breathe on her own.

She graduated to a pressurized mask, and later to prongs in her nose, which made her look even more like an old man on oxygen. She could close her mouth. She could suck her pacifier, which was smaller than a pencil eraser. And she could cry.

At first, her voice was tiny and hoarse. She mewled. It quickly strengthened, to a squeak like a rusty door hinge. During her weekly eye exams, when a doctor pried open her eyelids with metal clamps, she screamed. She screamed so loudly I had to step out into the hall and lean against the wall.

After two months of watching her writhe mutely, her cries were staggering. They were a testament not only to her will, but to the technology that had propped open her flimsy lungs until they could function.

Nearly 50 years ago, when John F. Kennedy's son was born at 34 weeks, there were no ventilators for preemies. The baby was placed in a high-pressure oxygen chamber—the newest technology—but lived just two days. If he were born today his odds of survival would be nearly 100 percent.

The death of baby Patrick Kennedy spurred innovation in neonatology. Early mechanical ventilation was tested on babies who had just died. Some sputtered briefly back to life.

In the late 1980s, artificial lung surfactant moved the limit of viability ahead several weeks. Babies like Juniper suddenly had a chance.

Juniper's lungs were scarred, maybe permanently. But her scratchy cry was a marvel. It was a triumph. It was an announcement.

People clash over the question of when life begins and when a fetus becomes a human being with its own standing and stake in the world. Some say it happens at conception. Some say it happens when the brain forms. I never saw my incomplete daughter as pre-human. Even on her first perilous day, four months before she was supposed to be born, I witnessed her individuality and her will. But there was something magical about watching her take shape in the incubator as she would have in my womb. When the ventilator came out, I saw that from under so much hardware, a little girl had emerged.

If she'd been born that day, in June, she would still have been two months premature. But she looked like a baby now, only smaller. She looked like one of those itty-bitty baby dolls toddlers drag around by the leg.

She had opinions. She felt pain, irritation, discontent, outrage.

For the first time, she had a voice.

Father's Day was approaching, and Tracy and I were plotting.

During slow periods at work, when Juniper was sleeping, Tracy took a piece of dark felt from her bag and cut it into two pieces shaped like a T. She hand-stitched it up both sides, and put a slit in the front for the wires. She was careful to hide the tiny robe when anyone was around, so she wouldn't ruin the surprise.

The other nurses were used to Tracy's stunts. She'd once dressed a baby in a blue top hat, bow tie, cummerbund and cuffs and tucked a tiny dollar bill into his diaper. A Chippen-preemie. There'd been a UPS driver, a nurse, and Rudolph the Red-nosed Reindeer. She'd wrapped one in gauze like a mummy in a haunted incubator, crawling with plastic spiders. The preemies always cooperated.

For the June telethon—"Pimpin' the preemies," Tracy called it—she'd decked out Juniper in her first real outfit. It was a black and white dress with a hot pink tutu and matching headband.

Where'd you find a dress that small? everyone asked. Tracy laughed. She got it in the pet aisle. It was made for a chihuahua.

Even in a place like this, it helped to maintain a sense of humor. But it was more than that. Tracy was starting to see Juniper react to things that could not be measured, prescribed or ordered on rounds. She breathed better when we were at her side. She responded to our stories and songs. Tracy was not sentimental. But she was starting to believe the risk she'd taken by letting herself get attached had been worth it.

When I watched Tracy lean close to Juniper and whisper, or stroke her head with a fingertip, or dress her up like a chihuahua at a dinner party, I knew she didn't just take care of my baby. She loved her.

Together one afternoon, Tracy and I broke the sticks from cotton swabs to make a tiny broomstick. Tracy had a superstition against dressing babies in eyeglasses, eye patches, fake casts, peg legs or anything that might portend a future disability. But this costume demanded round eyeglasses and a lightning bolt scar.

She cut out the glasses from a black hospital mask and drew the scar on a piece of clear tape. When the time came, just before Tom visited that afternoon, she stuck the scar on Juniper's forehead.

Harry Potter.

Like breathing, we say, as a metaphor for something effortless.

Now that the ventilator was out, it was all up to Juniper. It seemed so simple. In and out. In and out.

Sometimes she forgot.

One morning, very early before rounds, Juniper was blinking, looking around, holding Tom's finger. Then she was gray, limp, slumped. First her oxygen saturation started to drop, triggering one alarm. Then her heart rate dropped, and a more urgent alarm sounded. 150, 120, 80, 60, 40 . . .

Tom rubbed her back and stared at the monitor, then her face, the monitor, her face. "Come on baby."

Tracy hurried into the room. An alarm outside Juniper's door flashed red and a team swarmed in behind her. Juniper's lips were blue. Someone grabbed the green oxygen bag and held it to her face. Come on, Junebug, they were saying. Come on.

Long minutes passed before those numbers climbed again, the nurses stepped back, and Juniper glanced anxiously around the room, perhaps wondering where she had been.

This began happening up to a half dozen times a day. We saw numbers fall into single digits. Each time, I felt the room spin and my blood swoosh. There was nothing to do but retreat to a corner and try to stay on my feet.

Breathe, I would pray, plead, scream inside my head. Breathe.

This was common in very early babies, with their immature nervous systems. We saw it happen around us all the time. Sometimes it took just a pat on the back to bring Juniper back. Sometimes it took a team. It happened so often, the alarm light outside her door burned out.

Our night nurse, Kim Jay, began every evening with a quick prayer.

Please don't let her die on my shift.

I made a poster and stuck it on the wall of Juniper's room.

To Do:

X Survive birth

Breathe (ongoing)

X Heal tummy

X Win over Tracy

X 1000 grams

2000 grams

X Off the ventilator

Off oxygen

Lose chest tube

Dissolve blood clot

Learn to eat

Acquire pony

Tom added: Conquer space and time

I also posted a Freakout Level Indicator, color-coded. Most days were yellow—caution. Some days, like when she forgot to breathe, were orange. To get to green, she had to stop setting off the alarms. They said this would happen gradually, as she got older.

People still asked when she was coming home, and we had no answer. She had been in the hospital more than 100 days.

At home, I sat in the room that had once been the bedroom of Sam, my stepson. Now it was halfway to becoming a baby girl's nursery. The boy grease had been scrubbed from the baseboards. The paint had been touched up and the nail holes patched. I'd hung a Matisse print and put in a new dresser.

My husband said it was bad luck to keep decorating the nursery. I had to think about how it would feel to come home to this room if our baby died in the hospital. I decided that we were worthy parents, and one way or another, we would bring a baby into this house and into this room. Juniper deserved all the faith we could muster. If anything happened to her, we would try again, or adopt. We'd poke fate in the eye until fate gave in.

In one week that summer, two babies on our hall died. One was right next door. We saw the family tumble out of the room, shuddering and sobbing.

I walked past the room and peeked through the blinds. I saw the incubator in the dark, the baby under the sheet. The monitor was disconnected. A red light blinked on and off.

Every day our baby grew. Every day she was revealed to us. Every day we weighed our gratitude against the stubborn reality of a place where it is bad luck to look even one day ahead.

When Juniper was 3 months old and about 3 pounds, we got word that the blood clot in her heart had finally dissolved. The fluid in her chest had slowed to a dribble, then stopped. The chest tubes would soon be removed. She was beginning to outgrow the terrifying lapses in her breathing. The hole in her side had closed on its own, and she had started to poop into her diaper. It wasn't a guarantee that her intestines were healed and she would not need surgery later, but it was a great sign.

She could wear preemie clothes with the sleeves rolled up. She'd been moved out of the incubator into a real crib. We'd rushed to Target to buy a baby mobile. We could hold her almost as much as we wanted. When we spoke to her, she smiled. Not an insincere, half-hearted gassy smile. She beamed.

"You might want to buy a car seat," Diane said one afternoon. "She doesn't have too much left to accomplish here."

I'd waited months—no, years—for a reason to buy a car seat. Now, as Juniper's due date approached, Diane offered the first suggestion that she might leave the hospital.

All the rest of that day, Tom and I were a gloomy mess. Shaking and sometimes crying. Descending into silences.

"What is wrong with me?" Tom asked.

We took that night off from the NICU. We grabbed the dog, Muppet, and her beloved tennis ball, and headed to her favorite spot on earth, Fort De Soto beach.

It was a weeknight in July. We had the dog beach nearly to ourselves. The wind was strong and the waves were wrestling and racing each other to the shore. Muppet was all ears and tail and dancing feet.

Watching Muppet race down the beach, I realized why we'd come undone. For months, our coping mechanism had been to measure time in minutes and hours. We never looked ahead. We never had to deal with the colossal risk of expectation.

Now the sand was shifting. The hopes we had strangled for so long overwhelmed us.

The dog ran down the beach and back. Tom wrapped his arms around me and cried.

Aug. 3 arrived. My due date.

The date had been seared into my cortex, and reaching it felt like a milestone. But instead of a newborn I had a sick 4-month-old. I didn't know how to feel.

From now forward, my baby would have two ages: a real age and an adjusted age. Her birthday was 113 days ago, but developmentally she was at Day 1.

Our nurse that day, Carol Tiffany, could see the mix of emotions on my face. She sent a patient care assistant named Brooke to labor and delivery to fetch a bassinet. Then Brooke and I stripped Juniper to her birthday suit and wrapped her in one of those footprint blankets you see in every

Facebook photo of a new baby. We put a newborn hat on her head, and this time it fit. We weighed her—4 pounds 10 ounces. We took handprints and footprints. Diane signed a ceremonial fake birth certificate and Brooke put a sign on Juniper's crib: Happy Due Date to Me!

Brooke and I stood over my baby. Juniper had none of the doughy features of a newborn. She was lean and wise. She could easily push herself up on her forearms. She scanned the room and smiled.

I told Brooke about all the times I'd worried she would die.

Brooke nodded. Part of her job, it turned out, was helping parents who have lost a baby. She would make handprints and footprints for those parents too, and present them a hand-painted box.

"There were a few times they told me to get a box ready for Juniper, just in case."

When the blood drained out of my face, I tried not to let Brooke see me sway.

A few days later Juniper hit 5 pounds. I photographed her next to a sack of sugar. Dr. Aaron Germain pronounced her "officially almost boring." She had a setback after that, when fluid started building in her chest again. It would keep her in the hospital a couple more months, but everyone seemed to think that sooner or later she was headed home. She was transferred to the less critical side of the NICU, for "feeders and growers." Some nurses called it "slurpin' and burpin'. "

Here, Juniper had to learn to drink from a bottle. After being on a ventilator so long, she wanted nothing in her mouth. Tracy warned us she would probably go home on a feeding tube—lots of preemies did. I couldn't stand the thought of one more hole in her body. Her belly was gouged and pocked with scars.

Tom and I would hold her for hours, watching the turbulence flash across her face, then subside. We melted, like all new parents, at the sucking motions she made in her sleep. We passed on life advice that we'd handed down to her brothers.

Never hit a cop. Don't piss off Bob Dylan, because he will write a song about you.

We told her she did not need a man to take care of her. She was not a princess.

"You can be a warrior princess," Tom told her.

Eventually, with weeks of guidance and therapy, Juniper drank a few swallows from the bottle, then a few more. Kim, the night nurse, showed us how to support her chin with a finger and to twist the bottle when she slowed down, to remind her not to stop. Juniper projectile-vomited on Tom. We started having real baby moments, just like other people.

By then it was late August, and Juniper had been in the NICU longer than any of the other babies. Kim, who always made time to calm my nerves or listen to me fret, sat with me one night and reminded me that this place was supposed to be temporary. It was not a place for babies to grow up.

"You won't believe how she'll take off when you get her home," Kim said.

I could not imagine leaving this place, leaving behind the reassurances of the doctors, the nurses, the monitors. Who would take care of this baby? Who would take care of me?

"Will you come too?" I asked.

One night, after dark, Juniper started to gnaw on my shirt. Her meaning was clear. Everyone had said breast-feeding was probably out of the question, after all this time. She grew frantic, trying to eat the buttons off.

I would have given her anything. But my boob? I looked around like we were about to break a law, and then unbuttoned my shirt. She latched on. I heard her swallow.

It was exactly as weird as I'd imagined it would be.

"Kim!" I wailed. "What the hell?"

Kim smiled so big, she looked like she might cry.

When she was 5 months old, the prongs came out of Juniper's nose. We saw her face—her whole, bare face—with its big eyes, soft cheeks, red mouth, and startled look, like, why are you people crying?

The nurse told Juniper breathing was like riding a bike without training wheels. Tom told her the key was to keep her eyes on the road ahead, and feel the wind in her hair.

She kept going, going, going.

Not long after that, Nurse Carol helped me get Juniper ready for a bath. She whipped off her diaper, disconnected all the wires and handed me a naked baby.

"What are you doing?" I asked Carol. "She's off the monitors."

She was untethered for the first time in her life. What if I dropped her? Or she stopped breathing?

Nurse Carol had been doing this a long time.

"Are you watching your baby?" she said. "Just watch your baby."

She walked out.

In September, Nurse Kim started unhooking Juniper's monitor long enough for me to put her in a baby sling and walk the halls. We'd say *Hi* to all the babies as we passed their rooms. Jersey, Dontrell, I'mya, Freddy. There were always Miracles and Nevaehs—heaven spelled backward.

Juniper was outgrowing her room. She was outgrowing the hospital. She liked it when I walked fast.

Eventually I was allowed to carry her as far as the big window by the sixth-floor elevator. I held her up to it and let her look out at the lights and the moon and, in the distance, Tampa Bay.

"There's a big world out there," I told her. "I'm going to take you there."

I saw our reflection in the glass.

The doctor had tears in his eyes. He knew discharge day was near, so he'd approached us one afternoon as we were signing in at the front desk.

"I've worked here a long time, okay," Dr. Tony Napolitano said, "and there's such a thing as a miracle. And your baby is one."

Miracle. We had been hearing that word since the day of her birth. In those early awful days, I'd cringed. It was an overused, Hallmark cliche of a word, one that I'd banned from my writing, and, in general, my life. It was a word people used when the truth was so much more complicated.

Now, as our baby got ready to leave the hospital, I didn't mind the word. The people who said it spoke from experience and insight I didn't have.

On matters of faith, Tom and I have little clarity. But we were forced to consider the idea of a miracle.

I've spent months now with research and experts, and I know some things I wish I'd known when Juniper was born.

The odds we were given were correct: She had an 80 percent chance of death or significant disability. But there was another way of slicing the numbers that I had not considered. If she lived—as big an if as it was— her odds of being reasonably okay were about half.

And that first day when I was searching the statistics for loopholes, hoping to find an exemption for good parents, I would have been comforted to know that studies do show that babies with involved families have a huge advantage.

I'm not dismissing the possibility of miracles. Certainly Juniper defied medical expectation and astonished doctors who aren't easily moved. But it makes me uncomfortable to imagine it's as simple as God laying his lightning-bolt finger on our baby's head, passing over some other baby along the way. Passing over all those babies we saw lying under the sheets.

I only know that back in April, a young, inexperienced nurse looked at our baby at a critical moment and saw what machines had not seen. I know that one of the best nurses in the hospital risked her heart and went against her own judgment when she agreed to take Juniper on. I know a doctor facing an impossible decision looked into our baby's eyes and told God he was in control before ordering a risky surgery. I know the surgeon thought our baby was beyond repair, but somehow fixed her anyway. I know a 1-pound baby found the will to keep going day after day, until finally some version of the world that awaited her came into focus.

Maybe the miracle was all around us, in little pieces. The science that created her inside a petri dish from another woman's egg. The obstetricians who stalled my labor. The machine that breathed for her.

Tracy, with her attention to the smallest details. Diane, with her unwavering optimism. My husband, with his faithful reading from a 4,000-page story, and his belief that the ending was worth waiting for, and we'd all get there together.

Kim and all the other nurses who came running when I wailed. Who taught me to scrunch the diaper so it fit better, to pat her bottom to settle her for sleep. I had wondered, once, how to be a mother to a sci-fi baby in an artificial world. All those people taught me how. Juniper taught me how.

So if you want to say there's a miracle in any of that, I will say that feels true to me.

Tracy came to the hospital in the middle of her vacation. Kim came in with tears on her face. Dr. Shakeel lifted Juniper in her arms. Ana Maria, the Preemie Whisperer, gave her one last shoulder rub. Nurses, social workers, lactation consultants, respiratory therapists, patient care assistants and a trainee from gastroenterology all converged on our room in 6 North. Tom read from Chapter Seven of Book Seven of the Harry Potter series. Diane reminded us that she'd never doubted this day would come.

It was Oct. 25, 2011. Day 196.

Juniper wore a red tutu and a onesie that said, "Chico's Bail Bonds: Let Freedom Ring." Then she pooped all over that outfit, and Tracy orchestrated an emergency bath and produced from her big bag a homemade Harry Potter onesie. That was Tracy, pulling the answer out of her magic bag one more time. Finally Kim and Tracy disconnected the last of the wires and monitors.

We buckled Juniper into her car seat and carried her out. No wheelchair and no balloons, but that was okay. Tom and I walked side by side, Tracy beside us.

"She won't know which of us is her mom until we get to the car," I said to Tracy, not kidding.

In the elevator we negotiated who got to carry her out. (Him as far as the door, then me.) A couple in the elevator laughed at us. I wondered whether they were long-timers, like us. I wondered about the child they were tending to. My brain still played the game. Cystic fibrosis? Leaky heart? I remembered nights when I'd approach the building and look up at all the lighted windows, and wonder about the terrible things happening inside. Worlds ending. Holes in the universe, opening.

Now I knew something I hadn't known then. Tremendous things happened here every day too. They had been happening all this time, long before I had any reason to pay attention. This was our moment, but ours was not the only improbable child. The car seat went bump bump bump against my knee.

Juniper wore sunglasses, but I can't imagine what she must have made of it when those doors slid apart and everything opened up in front of her.

So much sun.

All that sky.

Epilogue

I still see the baby under the sheet.

If Tom wants to take Juniper with him to the grocery, I try to talk him out of it.

"Unnecessary risk," I say.

Until they return, images flash in my head. Ambulance lights. A crunched door panel. Shattered safety glass in the car seat.

Death breathed cold on her neck for months. Where did it go? Is it coming back? It always comes back.

It comes back.

She's 20 months old. But when people ask, I say she's 16 months old, because that's how old she would be if she'd been born on time. "So tiny!" they say. She weighs 18 pounds. Can't they see she's huge?

People ask if she's fine. I hesitate. The superstitions of the hospital have become part of me. I have learned how fast things go from fine to not fine. From fine to everything flying apart, everything unrecognizable, everything lost. Is she fine now? She's here. She's ours. She's magnificent.

She walks and runs. She does not need glasses. She feeds herself. Our ceiling is stained with blueberry yogurt. She sat up, crawled, took her first step, scrawled with crayon, all on schedule. The other day, I heard her laughing, spun around, and saw her standing naked on the coffee table, waving her diaper in the air.

She speaks in phrases: "I want that." "I did it." "I go there." About 500 times per day, she points at something and says "IZZAT!"

What's that! It's not a question.

She picks at her scars. Someday I will tell her how she earned each one. I can't guess how so many procedures and interventions might stunt her in the years ahead. Her brain was deprived of the proper fats for months; her body got too few calories. Time after time her oxygen levels plummeted. Did her brain suffer? Did her nerves get jangled? Does she remember pain? She is scrutinized by therapists and specialists. More than a year after leaving the hospital, she still has three to five appointments every week. Statistics say she's at risk for learning trouble, sensory issues, fine motor delays.

Statistics.

It's so quiet in her room. After I read to her and rock her and nurse her and feel her drift off in my arms, I hold her too long. I whisper to her the names of all the people who love her. Mommy, Daddy, Nat, Sam, Tracy, Diane, Dr. Shakeel, Kim, Ana Maria. . . . There are 30 or 40 names some nights. The doctors and nurses come before a lot of the family.

I kiss her, lower her into her crib, and forget to exhale.

I lay my hand on her back, feeling its rise and fall. Standing by her crib like that, it's so easy to imagine that she's back in that incubator. That I'm standing guard. That Tom is beside me in the blue chair. I note the ventilator settings. I hear the alarms. I watch her heart rate slow ever so gradually as she falls asleep. I stand there, just stand there.

I have to remind myself to come back to the present. To take in the crib, the dark room, the turning fan, the picture of Tracy on the bookshelf, the moonlight peeking through the blinds. No alarms, no wires, no machines. Just me and my daughter. My hand on her back. The soft steady whisper of a baby, breathing.

Breaking Free

The Washington Post

December 9, 2012, Suburban Edition

By Anne Hull

Week after week, the mailman climbed the steep hill of Shenango Street to the house with the busted porch steps. "Dear Miss Rouzzo," the letters began, or "Dear Tabitha Rouzzo." The college catalogues barely fit in the mailbox. They stuck out like gift-wrapped presents against white aluminum siding gone dingy from decades of wear. On the porch were three new Linen Breeze decorative candles—a nice try, thought the actual Tabitha Rouzzo, who came walking up the hill every afternoon with her mind on the mailbox.

The 11th-grader seldom brought anyone home, and when she did she would sort of draw in a breath and say, "Well, here it is."

Her Victoria's Secret bag was crammed with track clothes and school papers. At 17, with dark hair and dark eyes, she was a version of the actress Anne Hathaway if Anne Hathaway had stars tattooed on her hip, chipped blue nail polish and lived two blocks from the projects.

Tabi shared the rental house with her mother and sometimes her mother's boyfriend. Her four older siblings were grown. None of them had graduated from high school. They wore headsets and hairnets to jobs that were so futureless that getting pregnant at 20 seemed an enriching diversion. Born too late to witness the blue-collar stability that had once been possible, they occupied the bottom of the U.S. economy.

"I'm running from everything they are," she said.

The question was whether Tabi could outrun the odds against her.

She knew that colleges sent out millions of letters to 11th-graders who took the Princeton Review prep course. The whole Dear Tabitha campaign was about as personal as fliers from Tire Express. But nearing the end of her junior year of high school, without a single item of value to secure her future—not even a $50 U.S. savings bond from a departed relative—the mail was all she had.

So she sweated it out the old-fashioned way, joining Spanish Club, Chess Club, Bible Club, Art Club and the track team, where she may have been the worst pole-vaulter in the Pennsylvania-Ohio border region. On Wednesday nights, she was at church waving her praise hands in the air, and on Friday night, it was a school production of *No, No, Nanette*.

With no working vehicle at home, she had to walk most places. You could see her hoofing across the industrial landscape, her pink bag slung over her shoulder.

Tabi kept the college mail upstairs in her bedroom. She wrote back to 22 schools that offered biochemistry programs. Her goal was to be a forensic scientist in North Carolina. "It seems nice," Tabi said, though she had never been. She had never flown on an airplane. Her laptop was a second-hand PC she bought from a guy for $60. Her bedroom window overlooked a field strewn with Filet-O-Fish wrappers and Keystone Ice empties and, lower in the valley, the stacks at Ellwood Quality Steels chugging smoke.

Long before the recession, New Castle was a place of vanishing opportunity. It was 50 miles from Pittsburgh but felt farther, and while Steelers banners hung from awnings, the hard hat was a remnant of the past. Retail and food service jobs now outnumbered manufacturing jobs in the county. The top three employers were the hospital, state government and Liberty Mutual Insurance Company. Number seven was Wal-Mart, where Tabi's older brother worked in dairy until he was fired for stealing an energy drink.

Tabi heard stories about the olden days. She came from welders and ceramic production workers. But, to Tabi, the sprawling Shenango China factory where her grandfather and great-grandfather worked was just a boarded-up place on the way to Wal-Mart.

Her New Castle was the one that existed now: white, working class, with poverty that had deepened into the second and third generations. Nearly three-fourths of the students in Tabi's school qualified for free or reduced-price lunches, and one-third of New Castle families with children younger than 18 had incomes beneath the poverty level.

During the 2012 election, the campaigns of President Obama and Mitt Romney visited Pennsylvania a combined 38 times. With Ohio next door, the candidates and their wives barnstormed the region like few other places, focused almost entirely on the economy and strengthening the middle class. After the election, New Castle was still a hard town to be young and poor in.

They had $50 prepaid phones and $5 Day-Glo earbuds with the Chinese innards spilling out. They went to Township Tan for the 15-minute prom special. But the backwash of America's affluence was a dim substitute for the promise of the middle class, which had moved farther from their reach. The decline in economic mobility has made the bottom more difficult to climb up from.

Unlike her counterparts in higher ranges, prepped for ascension, Tabi Rouzzo had only herself.

At 13, she started working in a deer slaughterhouse. Her friend Gloria told her about it, and Gloria's mom drove them out there. They were greeted by a cold room with kerosene heaters. For $10 an hour, Tabi was to stand at a table cutting butterfly filets.

With a bloody knife in her hand and a circular saw whining behind her, labor laws being violated by the minute, Tabi decided on the spot that work offered freedom. She went back the next two winters, through 10th grade. Off-season, she cleaned rental properties, clerked in a mini-mart and baled hay at a farm.

In 11th grade, Tabi needed a job she could walk to and found Split-stone Entertainment, a storefront that sold used electronics, along with a selection of stun guns, nunchucks, ninja throwing stars and factory-boxed Star Wars collectibles. People brought in their Xboxes and PlayStations to unload, and Tabi cleaned them for resale.

"The controllers are real greasy," she said one Saturday afternoon, pulling back her hair for the task. She was not complaining. Even describing the slaughterhouse, she sounded like a butcher and not a squee girl. "I'm a grown man," she joked. It was somehow true. She had not a line on her porcelain face but a weariness was already in her.

After work that night, she met Gloria at Sheetz for dinner. Gloria was working midnights at the Subway inside the Pilot gas station for $8.60 an hour and was no longer in school.

"This town is dragging everyone down," Tabi said a few days later.

The mailbox at home remained a repository of hope. Tabi's mother brought the mail in every day. "She's got colleges all the way from Texas wanting her," said Patricia Edmonds, bragging about her daughter.

Tabi didn't spend much energy correcting the record. School, and her future, had always been hers to figure out.

Her mother had five kids and no husband at age 23. Tabi, the last born, was a welfare and WIC baby who grew up with evictions and lights getting cut off. Her 39-year-old mother remembers it differently.

"I tried to give them everything," Patricia said. "You wouldn't find one of my kids without a matching bed set."

Monthly income for Tabi and her mother at the house on Shenango Street was an $824 check from Social Security, food stamps and survivor's benefits for Tabi from the death of her father, a welder who died of an overdose. Patricia spent a lot of time on Facebook, posting shout-outs to her four grown children, "I'm cookin' sauce, you comin' home or what?" She listed herself as a "Stay at home mom" with a qualifier—"QueenBitch."

Tabi thought her mother should get a job. "I don't ever want to sit on my butt, waiting on hand and foot for someone to help me," Tabi said.

It was her greatest motivation. The college mail reminded her how badly she wanted to escape her mother's destiny. And yet the glossy pictures of emerald campuses revealed how far away that green world was.

Tabi's alarm for school went off at 5:45 a.m. It sounded like a firehouse bell, as if to stress the urgency of the moment. Tabi used to share the room with her older sister. One morning, Tabi's sister decided not to get up, and that was that for high school. Tabi pulled herself from bed.

The crowded halls of New Castle Junior/Senior High School enveloped her. "Yo, Tabs," a teammate from track called. Tabi wore khakis and ballet flats. The hard protective shell Tabi wore at home was gone.

Despite her aspirations, Tabi was not pushing herself at school. She rarely brought work home. Some of her teachers used class time to let students complete their assignments. If Tabi had extra homework, she blew through it at lunch. Even so, she maintained a 3.0 GPA while taking honors courses.

Four and five decades ago, when New Castle High was full of factory workers' kids, the school taught Chinese, Latin, German, Spanish, French and Italian. Now it was Spanish, French and Italian. As students became poorer, standards dropped lower. Tabi's junior year, the average SAT score was almost 200 points below the national average. To boost scores, the school has made the Princeton Review college prep course free for all sophomores during class hours. Private tutors are luxuries of a different solar system.

Tabi planned to take the SAT before the school year ended. She kept reminding herself to sign up.

She worked other angles. The annual science competition was coming up. In the ninth and 10th grade, Tabi made it to the final round, and she was hoping for a repeat performance and trip to Penn State.

"The main campus," Tabi said, as if speaking confidentially. "Maybe someone will see my project and help me get a scholarship."

What would have been nice was to be her friend Matt. He had an iPhone and two parents. They recently took Matt to visit Robert Morris University, a small liberal arts school outside Pittsburgh, and invited Tabi to come along.

A week later, in her school cafeteria, she was still talking about the trip. The campus tour was beautiful, and afterward, they met with an admissions counselor who estimated the cost of one year was $34,000. Tabi jumped in to warn Matt.

"I said, 'Matt, you're going to be paying off the loan for the rest of your life!' " she recounted at lunch. "His dad said, 'I think I got it covered.' "

There was more. On the way back to New Castle, they stopped for dinner at Olive Garden. Tabi couldn't help noticing the bill. "It was like $70!" Tabi said. "And it was no sweat off their back."

In the cafeteria, she went back to her free lunch and packed up for pre-calculus.

She needed to stop by the guidance office. At New Castle High, the office was the make-or-break room. It's where college-bound seniors stopped for applications—for loans, waivers, scholarships and grants. Mrs. Gibson, the senior guidance counselor, helped them fill out the paperwork. She also arranged etiquette dinners that taught proper grooming, eating and the do's and don'ts of dressing professionally.

But decorating the ceiling of the guidance counseling office was her most inspired idea.

It was a patchwork of college T-shirts. They were stapled across the entire ceiling. Each was autographed by a New Castle High grad who had gone on to glory: Slippery Rock University, Youngstown State University, Robert Morris University, Butler Community College, St. Vincent's College, Clarion University, Penn State and Pitt. The parachute hovered like a subliminal cloud: You can do it.

The deadline to sign up for the SAT came and went. Distracted, Tabi forgot.

Every Wednesday night, Tabi got a break from the hand-over-hand climbing that consumed her life.

She usually sat in the same spot: the front row, closest to the preacher. When Pastor Shawn told Tabi she would look back in 20 years and be blown away by all the things God had done for her, she hoped he was right.

But on one night, the chairs were cleared out. An inspirational thrash metal band was performing live at First Assembly of God. Half the teenagers in New Castle seemed to be going, Jesus-loving or not.

For years, Tabi rode the church bus that swept through New Castle's threadbare neighborhoods picking up poor kids. On the night of the concert, Tabi got an upgrade. Her friend Miranda gave her a ride. Traveling by private coach was the way to go.

Not a single space was left in the parking lot as the arrivals poured in —Tabi by car and the poor kids by bus. They tumbled down the stairs in a cloud of Sexiest Fantasies Body Spray. One girl was holding her MP3 player in the air like a transistor, the tiny rattling of Mindless Behavior's "Valentine's Girl" piping out through the 1-by-1-inch speaker.

Inside the church, God's abundance overflowed. Pastor Shawn had ordered enough pizzas and nachos to feed the Rust Belt. Shawn Galla, the 26-year-old youth pastor, had convinced church elders that a night of metal music and free prizes was more likely to bring in New Castle's teenagers than praise music and juice boxes.

Having grown up in working-class Pittsburgh with a single mother, Pastor Shawn thought he knew his audience when he took the job in New Castle in 2008, until he launched a fundraising drive for his kids and found their parents selling the Auntie Anne's pretzels for cash for themselves.

Tabi had inched her way to the front of the crowd when the lights went down and the screaming started. Pastor Shawn was on stage ready to start flinging CDs and McDonald's gift cards into the crowd.

"We're giving away free stuff!" he yelled. "EVEN JESUS!"

The band Icon for Hire was pierced and mohawked. "WHAT'S UP, NEW CASTLE!" the lead singer shouted, and the head banging commenced. The evening's motivational speaker, Seth Franco, a former Harlem Globetrotter, told his story of injury and comeback and invited anyone to raise their hands and come forward if they wanted to accept Jesus Christ.

"There's more to life than nothing," Seth said, as the electric keyboard softly lulled and the lights dimmed. "There's more to life than this town."

Words to Tabi's ears. She was not exceptionally pious and she had made her share of transgressions, but she always felt better at this moment when she closed her eyes and let go. The kids from the bus had their heads bowed, too. Some were wiping away tears, a few were sobbing, their shoulders heaving in the darkness of the church.

Then the lights blasted back on and Pastor Shawn was onstage, holding something small in his hand.

"WHO WANTS AN IPOD?"

The silver sporty coupe arriving at Tabi's one Saturday night was so polished and punctual that it made the sagging house sag a little more. The Dodge Stratus idled at the curb. Tabi came down the busted porch steps in a skirt.

In Deric Lewis she had a boyfriend with the right mix of qualities. "He has goals," Tabi said. "He's kinda smart. He works. He's always there five minutes early."

But he was also a source of tension in the house and had stopped going inside. Tabi's mother said Deric was a snob and was turning Tabi against her family. Tabi said that Deric was the best thing that ever happened to her. Opening the car door, she left her mother and "Storage Wars" behind.

Deric was 19 and smelled of soap. He worked full time at Castle Cheese, where he wore a hairnet in 100-degree heat reaching into milky buckets of mozzarella for $9.65 an hour. His dad was a scrap-metal worker. Determined to have an office job someday, Deric was a full-time student at the community college.

He and Tabi were headed for the outlet mall in Grove City, 30 miles away, to see if Deric could use a $20-off coupon he had at Aeropostale. Tabi leaned in close as he drove, until he yawned, and she punched him in the arm.

"Hey!" he said, laughing. He reminded her of his 6 a.m. shift that day. Tabi pointed out that she had also worked eight hours that day.

They were the oldest teenagers in America.

All around them in the rural dark, energy companies were buying up land for natural gas exploration. Deric heard in class that Shell Oil was building a $3 billion refinery site in Beaver County. There were millwright jobs across the border in Youngstown. Deric wondered if he was doing the right thing pursuing a business degree, which would take three more years of killing himself at the cheese plant.

Tabi thought school was the answer, and they should stick to the plan.

"We're lucky; we both work," she said, as they arrived at the outlet mall. "We have the advantage that others don't."

They held hands as they walked to Aeropostale. Deric didn't find anything. He folded the coupon and put it back in his wallet. Tabi took an armful of clothes into a dressing room. It was nice to try on new things.

"How'd those work out for you?" a saleswoman asked. Aeropostale would not be getting a dime of Tabi's money. The $124 in her purse— she was a fanatic about counting her cash—was going toward a trip to Chicago with the Spanish Club. She returned every item.

Back in New Castle, they drove around, killing time. High on a hill, the lights of the city blinked below, and in the pockets of darkness were the abandoned mausoleums of industry.

"They say money doesn't buy happiness, but I would love to be crying in my Porsche," Deric said.

Tabi's phone flashed with a text. Keys in the mailbox.

"Well, mom's going out," Tabi said, sounding both annoyed and apprehensive.

Later that night, Deric brought Tabi home to her dark patch of Shenango Street. She was almost to her front door when she heard her name being called. The woman was vaguely familiar, a neighbor, someone her mother maybe knew. She asked to borrow Tabi's phone. Then the woman asked for a glass of water. Tabi put her stuff down and went to the kitchen.

When she came back with the water, the woman was gone and so was Tabi's purse.

With crystal force, the stolen purse exposed the tension between Tabi and her mother, proven out in the weeks that followed.

Tabi partly blamed herself for responding to someone on the street at 1 in the morning. But she also blamed her mother for living in a neighborhood where people needed money at 1 in the morning.

For years, Tabi hid her cash in small stacks around her bedroom. Tabi was more flush than her mother. If her mom asked for a loan, Tabi charged 20 percent interest. Once, when her mom ran out of food stamps, Tabi, as if to impart a lesson, went out to eat.

Patricia Edmonds felt her daughter's judgment. Tabi was different from her other four. Patricia marveled at her as a spectator would, watching something rare and unexpected.

"She wants so much for herself," Patricia said.

Patricia hung Tabi's awards on the living room wall. The sprawling constellation gave Patricia a tangible sense of accomplishment.

In her face and spirit were traces of the cheerleader who got pregnant in the eighth grade. Patricia's father was a welder and her mother a nurse's aide. The love of her life was a dark-haired welder named Frankie Rouzzo, Tabi's father. They had two daughters and Tabi on the way when they split. He died when Tabi was 10, and since then Patricia had maintained a fragile livelihood on the survivor's benefits for her three daughters.

She tried pleasing her vegetarian daughter, buying Tabi her favorite chocolate soy milk and making special trips to Wal-Mart for the bags of lettuce Tabi liked. "I made her Taco Bell Grande with tofu meat," Patricia said.

But Tabi had withdrawn. She came home from track practice, poured some lettuce on a plate, doused it in ranch and took her dinner upstairs.

The explosion happened on a Saturday night. Patricia was bigger, badder and louder than Tabi. But Tabi had resentment that went back years.

She said Deric hadn't brainwashed her against her family; the feelings were entirely her own. There was a difference between bad luck and bad choices, Tabi said, and she had grown up captive of her mother's choices.

"You think you're better then me, don't you?" Patricia yelled. "I had five kids!"

"Mom," Tabi yelled back, "you quit school. Does it dawn on you after your first [child] not to have a second one?"

It was a lethal blow, as only a teenage girl could deliver. Patricia got pregnant in the eighth grade, the same age Tabi was when she started at the slaughterhouse.

Patricia grounded Tabi for a month. She confiscated her phone—which Deric had paid for—and banned all activities except school and work.

One day after school, Tabi went to see her Uncle Bill about moving in with him. He worked at the jail and was a steady presence. When Tabi was 10, she went to stay with him when her mom was in a period of chaos. He took her to violin lessons.

Standing on the sidewalk at Uncle Bill's, the sun beat down. Tabi and her uncle and his wife were quiet.

"What are you gonna do?" Bill said, still in his jail uniform.

"It's up to you, Tab," Sybil said.

Tabi left their house on foot. She took the broken sidewalk that led her downtown. The beige mannequins and the Coney Island, the old motor lodge and legal disability clinic, Tabi hardly looked up.

"If I move out, my mom would lose the check, lose everything," Tabi said, weighed down by the decision.

When she reached home, it was different. Pine scent wafted. Folded stacks of laundry sat on the couch. The cleaning spree went on all week. Patricia went room to room, carrying out bags to the curb and posting her progress on Facebook. She was serious about taking a course in emergency medical technician training.

Patricia declared she was turning it around. Tabi had heard it before. But this time, her mother made a promise and extracted one from Tabi—she had to break up with Deric.

Wanting to believe, Tabi agreed.

On a Saturday morning in June, Tabi walked to school to take the SAT. She had remembered to sign up for this one. Five interminable hours later, it was over, and Tabi went to work.

Summer without Deric was empty. There were grimy Xboxes to clean at Splitstone and swimming at the rock quarry. On Friday nights, Tabi and a friend hung out at a convenience store where a handwritten sign on the beverage station said, in friendly curlicue, "Smoothies, Slushies and Fountain pops cannot be bought with food stamps!"

Tabi got her first plane ride—a church mission to Guatemala.

When school started in the fall, senior year felt different. An hourglass had been turned and the sand was falling. The college buzz greeted Tabi in the hallways, and it gave her the feeling that she was somehow already behind.

"Everybody's asking, 'Where are you going?' " Tabi said. "That worries me I don't have it figured out."

Applications to fill out, deadlines to meet—it all hovered. Her SAT results were not what she hoped. They were above the average score at New Castle but well shy of the national median.

But Tabi, a master of contingency, already had a Plan B. On top of school, she started night classes to get certified as an EMT. True to her promise, her mother enrolled, too, and they sat side by side, sharing Tabi's textbook.

Patricia, who had not been in a classroom since eighth grade, spent afternoons at the public library. She and Tabi left Shenango Street for a new rental house, funded with help from Patricia's boyfriend.

Buried in school, work and EMT training, Tabi began to recalibrate.

The Navy recruiter was in the cafeteria at school when a 17-year-old girl approached. She was ready to sign her name—Tabitha Rouzzo. She didn't want to hear a pitch. Tabi had learned enough online about a reservist's pay and travel. College could wait. When it did start, tuition would be on the Navy and Tabi would be gone from New Castle.

Snowfall: The Avalanche at Tunnel Creek

The New York Times

By John Branch

The snow burst through the trees with no warning but a last-second whoosh of sound, a two-story wall of white and Chris Rudolph's piercing cry: "Avalanche! Elyse!"

The very thing the 16 skiers and snowboarders had sought—fresh, soft snow—instantly became the enemy. Somewhere above, a pristine meadow cracked in the shape of a lightning bolt, slicing a slab nearly 200 feet across and 3 feet deep. Gravity did the rest.

Snow shattered and spilled down the slope. Within seconds, the avalanche was the size of more than a thousand cars barreling down the mountain and weighed millions of pounds. Moving about 70 miles per hour, it crashed through the sturdy old-growth trees, snapping their limbs and shredding bark from their trunks.

The avalanche, in Washington's Cascades in February, slid past some trees and rocks, like ocean swells around a ship's prow. Others it captured and added to its violent load.

Somewhere inside, it also carried people. How many, no one knew.

The slope of the terrain, shaped like a funnel, squeezed the growing swell of churning snow into a steep, twisting gorge. It moved in surges, like a roller coaster on a series of drops and high-banked turns. It accelerated as the slope steepened and the weight of the slide pushed from behind. It slithered through shallower pitches. The energy raised the temperature of the snow a couple of degrees, and the friction carved striations high in the icy sides of the canyon walls.

Elyse Saugstad, a professional skier, wore a backpack equipped with an air bag, a relatively new and expensive part of the arsenal that backcountry users increasingly carry to ease their minds and increase survival odds in case of an avalanche. About to be overtaken, she pulled a cord near her chest. She was knocked down before she knew if the canister of compressed air inflated winged pillows behind her head.

She had no control of her body as she tumbled downhill. She did not know up from down. It was not unlike being cartwheeled in a relentlessly crashing wave. But snow does not recede. It swallows its victims. It does not spit them out.

Snow filled her mouth. She caromed off things she never saw, tumbling through a cluttered canyon like a steel marble falling through pins in a pachinko machine.

At first she thought she would be embarrassed that she had deployed her air bag, that the other expert skiers she was with, more than a dozen of them, would have a good laugh at her panicked overreaction. Seconds later, tumbling uncontrollably inside a ribbon of speeding snow, she was sure this was how she was going to die.

Moving, roiling snow turns into something closer to liquid, thick like lava. But when it stops, it instantly freezes solid. The laws of physics and chemistry transform a meadow of fine powder into a wreckage of icy chunks. Saugstad's pinwheeling body would freeze into whatever position it was in the moment the snow stopped.

After about a minute, the creek bed vomited the debris into a gently sloped meadow. Saugstad felt the snow slow and tried to keep her hands in front of her. She knew from avalanche safety courses that outstretched hands might puncture the ice surface and alert rescuers. She knew that if victims ended up buried under the snow, cupped hands in front of the face could provide a small pocket of air for the mouth and nose. Without it, the first breaths could create a suffocating ice mask.

The avalanche spread and stopped, locking everything it carried into an icy cocoon. It was now a jagged, virtually impenetrable pile of ice, longer than a football field and nearly as wide. As if newly plowed, it rose in rugged contrast to the surrounding fields of undisturbed snow, 20 feet tall in spots.

Saugstad was mummified. She was on her back, her head pointed downhill. Her goggles were off. Her nose ring had been ripped away. She felt the crushing weight of snow on her chest. She could not move her legs. One boot still had a ski attached to it. She could not lift her head because it was locked into the ice.

But she could see the sky. Her face was covered only with loose snow. Her hands, too, stuck out of the snow, one still covered by a pink mitten.

Using her hands like windshield wipers, she tried to flick snow away from her mouth. When she clawed at her chest and neck, the crumbs maddeningly slid back onto her face. She grew claustrophobic.

Breathe easy, she told herself. Do not panic. Help will come. She stared at the low, gray clouds. She had not noticed the noise as she hurtled down the mountain. Now, she was suddenly struck by the silence.

TUNNEL CREEK

The Cascades are among the craggiest of American mountain ranges, roughly cut, as if carved with a chain saw. In summer, the gray peaks are sprinkled with glaciers. In winter, they are smothered in some of North America's deepest snowpack.

The top of Cowboy Mountain, about 75 miles east of Seattle, rises to 5,853 feet—about half the height of the tallest Cascades, but higher than its nearest neighbors, enough to provide 360-degree views. It feels more like a long fin than a summit, a few feet wide in parts. Locals call it Cowboy Ridge.

To one side, down steep chutes, is Stevens Pass ski area, which receives about 400,000 visitors each winter. To the other, outside the ski area's boundary to what is considered the back of Cowboy Mountain, is an unmonitored play area of reliably deep snow, a "powder stash," known as Tunnel Creek.

It is a term with broad meaning. The name is derived from the Cascade Tunnel, originally a 2.6-mile railroad tube completed in 1900 that connected the east and west sides of the Cascades, a boon for the growth of Seattle and Puget Sound. The mountain pass that it burrowed beneath was named for the project's engineer, John Frank Stevens, who later helped build the Panama Canal.

In late February 1910, ceaseless snowstorms over several days marooned two passenger trains just outside the tunnel's west portal. Before the tracks could be cleared, the trains were buried by what still stands as the nation's deadliest avalanche. It killed 96 people.

Bodies were extricated and wrapped in blankets from the Great Northern Railway, then hauled away on sleds. Some were not found until the snow melted many months later.

To skiers and snowboarders today, Tunnel Creek is a serendipitous junction of place and powder. It features nearly 3,000 vertical feet—a rarely matched descent—of open meadows framed by thick stands of trees. Steep gullies drain each spring's runoff to the valley floor and into a small, short gorge called Tunnel Creek.

The area has all of the alluring qualities of the backcountry—fresh snow, expert terrain and relative solitude—but few of the customary inconveniences. Reaching Tunnel Creek from Stevens Pass ski area requires a ride of just more than five minutes up SkyLine Express, a high-speed four-person chairlift, followed by a shorter ride up Seventh Heaven, a steep two-person lift. Slip through the open boundary gate, with its "continue at your own risk" warning signs, and hike 10 minutes to the top of Cowboy Mountain.

When snow conditions are right, the preferred method of descent used by those experienced in Tunnel Creek, based on the shared wisdom passed over generations, is to hopscotch down the mountain through a series of long meadows. Weave down the first meadow, maybe punctuate the run with a jump off a rock outcropping near the bottom, then veer hard left, up and out of the narrowing gully and into the next open glade.

Another powder-filled drop ends with another hard left, into another meadow that leads to the valley floor.

Tunnel Creek is, in the vernacular of locals, a "hippie pow run"—breezy and unobstructed, the kind that makes skiers giggle in glee as they descend through a billowing cloud of their own soft powder and emerge at the bottom coated in white frosting.

Despite trends toward extreme skiing (now called freeskiing), with improbable descents over cliffs and down chutes that test the guile of even the fiercest daredevils, the ageless lure of fresh, smooth powder endures.

But powder and people are key ingredients for avalanches. And the worry among avalanche forecasters, snow-science experts and search-and-rescue leaders is that the number of fatalities—roughly 200 around the world each year—will keep rising as the rush to the backcountry continues among skiers, snowboarders, climbers and snowmobilers.

The backcountry represents the fastest-growing segment of the ski industry. More than ever, people are looking for fresh descents accessible by helicopters, hiking or even the simple ride up a chairlift.

Before 1980, it was unusual to have more than 10 avalanche deaths in the United States each winter. There were 34 last season, including 20 skiers and snowboarders. Eight victims were skiing out of bounds, legally, with a lift ticket. And many of the dead were backcountry experts intimate with the terrain that killed them.

"It's a cultural shift, where more skiers are going farther, faster, bigger," said John Stifter, the editor of *Powder* magazine, who was a part of the group at Tunnel Creek in February. "Which is tending to push your pro skiers or other experienced, elite-level backcountry skiers that much farther, faster and bigger, to the point where there's no margin for error."

No one knows how many avalanches occur. Most naturally triggered slides are never seen. Those set off by humans are rarely reported unless they cause fatalities or property damage.

But avalanches occur in Tunnel Creek regularly. Its slopes, mostly from 40 to 45 degrees, are optimal for avalanches—flat enough to hold deep reservoirs of snow, yet steep enough for the snow to slide long distances when prompted. The long elevation drop means snow can be fluffy at the top and slushy at the bottom. Temperatures, wind and precipitation change quickly, and something as welcome as a burst of sunshine can alter the crystallized bonds deep inside the snow. And because Tunnel Creek is outside the ski area, it is not patrolled or specifically assessed for danger.

In March 2011, a University of Washington student was caught in an avalanche in Tunnel Creek. Having been carried into a stand of trees, he was unburied by friends within minutes and found dead. Three others were partially buried about an hour later when the ski patrol's arrival set off a second avalanche.

Many of the most experienced locals view Tunnel Creek with a mix of awe and fear.

"I've always been a naysayer of Tunnel Creek," the snowboarder Tim Wesley said. "I've seen a big avalanche back there before. It has about 2,600 vertical feet. Not typical. The snow changes a lot in that distance. That's the reason I always have a second thought about Tunnel Creek. In Washington, there's a saying: If you don't like the weather, wait five minutes. And it's true. You'll be on the chair and it'll be freezing, and then all of a sudden there's a warm breeze that smells like the ocean."

Even those who are not leery of Tunnel Creek on the best days heed the pass-it-on warning of the experienced: stay left.

To head straight down to the bottom is to enter what experts call a terrain trap: a funnel of trouble and clumsy skiing, clogged with trees and rocks and confined by high walls. Few go that way intentionally.

Chris Rudolph, the effervescent 30-year-old marketing manager for Stevens Pass, knew the preferred route down. Tunnel Creek was his favorite at-work diversion. Earlier that weekend, he mentioned plans for a field trip to Tunnel Creek to a select group of high-powered guests and close friends.

The operations manager for Stevens Pass agreed to pick up the group in one of the ski area's trucks at the end of its descent. From the bottom of Tunnel Creek, it is about a half-mile trek through deep snow to U.S. 2, then a four-mile ride back to Stevens Pass.

At 11:32 a.m. on Sunday, Feb. 19, heading up the mountain, Rudolph sent a text message to the operations manager.

"A big posse," Rudolph wrote.

A PLAN IN MOTION

Like many ideas that sound good at the time, skiing Tunnel Creek was an idea hatched in a bar.

It was Saturday, Feb. 18, the afternoon light fading to dusk. Outside the Foggy Goggle, a bar at the base of the ski area, the snow continued to fall, roughly an inch an hour. By morning, there would be 32 inches of fresh snow at Stevens Pass, 21 of them in a 24-hour period of Saturday and Saturday night.

That was cause for celebration. It had been more than two weeks since the last decent snowfall. Finally, the tired layer of hard, crusty snow was gone, buried deep under powder.

Rudolph promoted Stevens Pass with restless zeal. In seven years there, he helped turn a relatively small, roadside ski area into a hip destination.

He unabashedly courted ski journalists and filmmakers to take a look. They, in turn, gave Stevens Pass star turns in magazines and popular ski movies, raising the area's cool quotient.

Rudolph was the oldest of three children raised in California's Bay Area by outdoors-minded parents. The young family pulled a pop-up Coleman camper around the West and skied the areas around Lake Tahoe. The grown siblings continued to vacation with their parents, climbing peaks like Mount Whitney in California and Mount Rainier in Washington.

Rudolph peppered his language with words like "rad" and "stoked." But he was no simple-minded ski bum. He was an Eagle Scout with a marketing degree. When he applied at Stevens Pass years earlier, he sent a video of himself speaking, skiing and mountain biking. He included a bag of popcorn for the viewer. He got the job.

Children knew Rudolph because he kept his pockets full of Stevens Pass stickers. He starred in self-deprecating Webcasts promoting Stevens Pass.

He wrote poetry on his blog and strummed a guitar. He drank Pabst Blue Ribbon, the unofficial beer of irony and the hipster generation.

Tunnel Creek was where he took special guests. And it is where he wanted to take the tangled assortment of high-caliber skiers and industry insiders who, as if carried by the latest storm, had blown into Stevens Pass that weekend.

Many of them happened into the Foggy Goggle on Saturday night.

Among them were professional skiers like Saugstad, 33, a former champion of the Freeride World Tour. There were reporters and editors from *Powder* magazine and ESPN. There were executives from ski equipment and apparel companies. There were Stevens Pass regulars, some with broad reputations in the niche world of skiing, glad to spend time with the assortment of guests.

"It was a very, very deep, heavy, powerful, strong group of pro skiers and ski industry people," said Keith Carlsen, a photographer and former editor of *Powder*.

Rudolph was the connecting thread. Some visitors, like Saugstad, were at Stevens Pass for a promotional event aimed at expert female skiers, sponsored by Salomon, the ski equipment maker. Rudolph skied with the group all day Saturday. He organized and hosted a catered dinner for the women later that night in Leavenworth, a serious outdoors town dressed as a Bavarian village, 35 miles downhill to the east.

Powder had come to spotlight Stevens Pass for a feature article on night skiing. When the magazine's editor, John Stifter, arrived by train to Leavenworth two days earlier, he found Rudolph's car waiting for him. Inside were keys to the car, keys to a slope-side cabin and two Pabst Blue Ribbons in the cup holders.

At the bar, Rudolph mentioned an idea to a few people: Tunnel Creek on Sunday. Invitations traveled in whispers and text messages, through a knot of friendships and slight acquaintances.

Meet at the fire pit, on the stone deck at Granite Peaks Lodge, at 11. Rudolph thought his Sunday morning staff meeting would end by then.

As darkness enveloped Stevens Pass on Saturday night, stadium-style lights flooded the slopes in white light, and snowflakes fell in cotton-ball clumps.

Rudolph and those with the Salomon event left for dinner in Leavenworth. Stifter, 29, and Carlsen, 38, headed outside to work on their article for *Powder*.

"I skied just off the trail, not out of bounds, but in the ski resort, to shoot some of these night shots I took," Carlsen said. "And in tree wells I was, like, neck deep—easily nipple deep, wading around in snow, trying to get my angle. There was so much new snow."

With the daytime crowds gone, the nighttime atmosphere was festive and the faces were familiar. Families played in the deepening snow. More serious skiers and snowboarders sought the freshest powder.

There are no public accommodations at Stevens Pass, only a parking lot available to a few dozen campers and recreational vehicles. As the evening wound down, several of those with loose plans to ski Tunnel Creek the next morning huddled in the R.V. lot around a fire. Carlsen continued taking photographs. Stifter and others ducked inside one camper to watch homemade videos of others skiing Tunnel Creek over the past couple of decades.

"So it's something they skied often," Stifter said. "Not something like, 'We're going to go ski Tunnel!' Not like a once-a-year deal."

The flames in the fire died to orange embers. The last beers were sipped empty, and people slipped into the night. The campers were blanketed with snow.

Beyond the lights glowing from the ski area, snow still fell over the ridge, too, in the vast darkness of steep meadows and narrow gullies just past the western edge of Stevens Pass.

Each snowflake added to the depth, and each snowflake added to the weight. It might take a million snowflakes for a skier to notice the difference. It might take just one for a mountain to move.

To the Peak

Dawn cracked with the intermittent sound of explosives near the top of Cowboy Mountain. Stevens Pass ski patrollers, called to duty whenever more than a few inches of snow fell, had arrived to check and control the ski area's 200 inbounds avalanche zones.

After getting the latest assessment from the area's full-time avalanche forecaster, more than a dozen patrollers filled their backpacks with 2.2-pound emulsion charges, shaped like cartoon dynamite. Chairlifts rumbled to life, ferrying the crews up the dark mountain.

Three two-person teams assigned to Cowboy Ridge removed their skis and filed through the boundary gate. They took turns plowing a path through the fresh snow with their bodies. Their boots forged an icy stairway to the top of the skinny ridge.

Back on their skis, facing down into the ski area and with their backs to Tunnel Creek, they spread across the ridge to stamp and destroy wind-swept cornices, small balconies of crusty snow.

They removed the charges from their packs. Like party poppers that spew confetti, charges have a pull-wire, an ignition that lights a 90-second fuse. The patrollers lobbed the lighted charges into the many steep chutes below them. With muffled booms, heavy waves of snow tumbled harmlessly into the recesses of the empty slopes below, clearing danger for the day's thousands of inbounds customers.

The lines for the ski lifts began forming about 7, two hours before they were to open. When the gathering skiers and snowboarders heard the explosions echo down the mountain, they cheered. It signaled a powder day.

In Leavenworth, Chris Rudolph awoke in his two-bedroom house on Ash Street, the one that he and his girlfriend, Anne Hessburg, painted a rich blue and accented with a garden out front.

"Chris was so mad that he had a meeting," Hessburg said. "It was a pow day, and you couldn't tie him to his desk on pow days."

But he thought the meeting would end by 11.

"He said: 'It's going to be so good, babe. I'm going to take some folks up to Tunnel Creek,'" Hessburg said. "Tunnel Creek, it was kind of like the holy grail for Chris. It was where he wanted to show off for friends."

Among those who joined the 45-minute parade from Leavenworth, through tight Tumwater Canyon, past the Lake Wenatchee turnoff and up to Stevens Pass, were Dan Abrams and Megan Michelson. They planned to marry in March.

Michelson, 30, was the freeskiing editor for ESPN.com. Abrams, 34, was a founder and the president of Flylow, maker of apparel marketed to backcountry users.

The couple lived in Seattle, but had come to Stevens Pass on Saturday for the Salomon promotional event. Michelson and the other women stayed at a Leavenworth hotel. Abrams slept in a spare bedroom at Rudolph's house. He and Michelson drove to Stevens Pass together.

"I said to Dan, 'Do you think Tunnel will be safe today?'" Michelson said. "He said something along the lines of, 'Yeah, those guys know the best route down.'"

There were similar conversations elsewhere. In the slope-side cabin at Stevens Pass that Rudolph arranged—he cleaned it on Friday as he spoke to his mother on the phone—the journalists from *Powder* magazine, Stifter and Carlsen, contemplated the day's plans.

"We started asking questions," Carlsen said. " 'Where are we going? Out of bounds? Didn't it just snow nonstop for two days? How much snow?' That's when John pulled up the avalanche report, and he read it aloud."

Mark Moore, director and lead meteorologist of the Northwest Weather and Avalanche Center, had set that day's forecast on Saturday afternoon. A 64-year-old with graying hair pulled into a short ponytail, Moore had a feeling it could be a busy weekend.

The avalanche center, based in Seattle, is one of about 20 regional avalanche forecasting centers in the United States, most run by the Forest Service. During the winter, one of its three employees arrives in the middle of the night, analyzes weather maps and computer models, and examines data — snowfall, temperatures, wind, humidity and so on — from 47 remote weather stations scattered across the mountains, including five in the vicinity of Stevens Pass. They take calls from ski patrollers and highway crews.

The biggest storm of the season increased avalanche concerns. But it was not just the new snow that concerned Moore. It was what lay nearly three feet beneath—a thin layer of perfectly preserved frost called surface hoar. The frozen equivalent of dew, created on crisp, clear nights, it features fragile, featherlike crystals that grow skyward.

On the surface, they glimmer like a million tiny diamonds. When frosted and protected by soft blankets of fluffy snow, they are weak stilts supporting all that falls on top. When they finally give way, falling like microscopic dominoes on a steep slope, they provide an icy flume for the snow above.

A shot of rain or above-freezing temperatures, both common in Cascade winters, usually destroy the fragile crystals, melding them into the snowpack. But five days of dry, cold weather, from Feb. 3 to 7, created a perfect, sparkly layer of surface hoar. Sporadic light snow, never more than an inch or two a day, delicately shrouded it over the next 10 days.

By the weekend, as snow fell heavily over the Cascades and powder-hungry hordes took to the slopes, the old layer was long out of sight, and mostly out of mind.

Not to Moore.

"Snowpack is never static," he said. "It's changing, even once it's buried."

Changes in temperatures, precipitation, humidity and wind can turn a benign snowpack into a deadly one, and vice versa. Sometimes weather is enough to start an avalanche. But "natural" avalanches rarely kill. The majority of avalanche fatalities are in human-triggered slides—usually of the victims' own making.

"Every skier, everyone who hits the slope, changes the structure of the snowpack," Moore said. "Even though they don't know it."

In the rugged area of the Cascades that includes Stevens Pass, Moore deemed the avalanche danger "high"—the fourth degree out of five—for slopes above 5,000 feet in elevation, facing north to southeast.

For everything else, the danger level was deemed "considerable," defined as "dangerous avalanche conditions" with "human-triggered avalanches likely."

The top of Cowboy Mountain is nearly 6,000 feet. The Tunnel Creek terrain descends off its southwest side to roughly 3,000 feet. Officially, the danger was "considerable."

"In avalanche forecasting terms, 'considerable' is a really weird fore-cast," Saugstad said. "Because it's this gray area. It's a hard one to predict. It can mean, well, you're not going to see any activity. Or, if something goes, you're going to be screwed. It's hard to work with that one."

Moore's forecast offered more specifics.

"Although decreasing light showers and decreasing winds are expected Sunday, cold temperatures should slow stabilization of existing wind slabs and help maintain the threat of further human-triggered avalanche activity, especially on previously wind-loaded terrain showing no evidence of recent avalanche activity," Moore wrote.

Spotty afternoon sunshine, he added, could raise the danger, especially on south-facing slopes.

The snow had stopped at Stevens Pass by the time the lifts opened Sunday morning. The runs were quickly doodled with curvy lines.

Stifter sat in the cabin and examined the forecast on his laptop.

"I have this image burned in my head," Stifter said. "I had a coffee cup in my right hand, I was reading e-mails, and I read the Northwest Avalanche Center report. And it said 'considerable to high' was the avalanche danger. And I read it out loud to Keith. And he listened, and I read it again—I read it twice—and looked at it. Huh. I've skied enough to know that when it snows a lot, which it did, up to two feet, there's always going to be instability, with that much weight on an older snowpack."

Stifter left Carlsen behind and headed to the lifts. He found Jim Jack. If anyone could judge terrain and snow in the backcountry, it was Jim Jack.

The license plate on Jack's Subaru Brat as a teenager read "IM JIM." To family and his closest friends, he was Jimmy, sometimes J. J. To most everyone else, he was Jim Jack, blended into one name, accent on the first syllable: JIM-jack.

Jack was the head judge and former president of the International Freeskiers Association, which oversaw a world tour of competitions. At 46, he was a sort of Peter Pan of the ski world, a charismatic, carefree boy who never grew up, beloved by like-minded skiers and snowboarders half his age.

He spent winters traveling the world, spreading the gospel of freeskiing, professing the beauty of finding improbable ways down precarious slopes with grace, nerve and flair. He had been a competitor on the tour, distinguishable from great distances by the silkiness of his loose form, until he landed hard and took his own knee to his face, shattering the bones around his right eye. You could feel the screws when you touched his face.

He was a party accelerator with a penchant for streaking. He did drama in high school and never declined the stage as an adult. On Halloween, his costumes played off his name: Jack on the Rocks, Jim Jack in the Box, Cracker Jack, Jack Frost.

Wearing lederhosen, Jack starred in a cheeky promotional video for Leavenworth. He was a sure-handed shortstop for the team from Uncle Uli's, a bar and restaurant in the heart of town. A grilled chicken sandwich on the menu, smothered in spicy sauce, is named the Napkin' Slappin' Jim Jack.

Jack shared a bungalow off the highway, near the Howard Johnson, with his longtime girlfriend, Tiffany Abraham. They danced late at night in the kitchen and built bonfires in the backyard. The covered front porch held a pile of ski gear and a futon couch, perfect for watching the world go by, beer in hand.

Jack drove a 1994 Chevy pickup with 216,000 miles on it, topped by a Wilderness camper that he added for $350. Widely recognized on the highways and in ski area parking lots around the West, it was held together largely by duct tape and bungee cords. The radio's volume was stuck on high. If it is too loud, Jack told passengers, just roll down the window.

Jack and his camper rolled into the R.V. parking lot at Stevens Pass on Friday night. On weekends, when the snow was good, the lot filled with dozens of pickup campers and motor homes.

"I woke up on Saturday in my R.V.," said Tim Wangen, a 53-year-old former commercial diver who lived in a cabin at nearby Lake Wenatchee.

"When I wake up, I look outside to see who is next to me. I saw that Jim Jack was next to me. I thought, cool, I got a great neighbor this week."

Jack and Wangen had skied a couple of runs Sunday morning by the time Stifter caught up to them. Wangen knew Tunnel Creek as well as anyone, having skied it since he was a boy. Jack traveled the world, scouting courses for extreme skiing. He knew how to avoid danger.

Stifter asked Jack about the avalanche report.

"He's like: 'Yeah, not to worry,' " Stifter said. "'We'll just do it slowly and safely and just stay in the trees.'"

"GEAR UP?"

The fire pit sits at the center of the bustle on busy days. At the corner of the patio, in front of the lodge, it is a crossroads for people coming and going. Some pull up chairs and relax, facing the bowl of ski runs strung before them. When the clouds lift, Cowboy Mountain dominates the view high to the right. It can feel close enough to reach and touch.

By midmorning, the fire pit began attracting a growing but confused band of expert skiers. Some were local, some were visitors. Some knew others, some did not, but most knew either Chris Rudolph or Jim Jack. They traded nods and handshakes, unsure if others were headed to Tunnel Creek, too.

"We didn't know why everyone was there," said Dan Abrams, there with Megan Michelson. "We wondered if everyone was meeting up for the same reason. But it's like when you find out where the extra keg is at the party. You don't go tell everybody."

Joel Hammond, the 37-year-old regional sales representative for Salomon, had teamed with Rudolph to organize the previous day's women's event. He did not intend to ski Sunday until he awoke in Leavenworth and could not resist the lure of the fresh snow. He drove to Stevens Pass and sent a text message to Rudolph, still in a staff meeting.

"Chris was like: 'Meet at the fire pit, where everybody meets. Then we're going to rally up,' " Hammond said.

Hammond told Jack that he had the latest model of skis in his truck, then left to retrieve a pair for him to try. Stifter bought coffee, a couple of Americanos, from the stand for himself and Jack.

Tim Carlson and Ron Pankey, both 37 and childhood friends from Vermont, had spent the morning on the inbounds side of Cowboy Mountain, navigating near-vertical chutes and rock outcroppings. During a break, they spotted familiar faces near the fire pit.

Pankey was a former competitor on the Freeskiing World Tour, so he had known Jack since the mid-1990s. Like Jack, he eventually worked competitions around the world, including the X Games.

Carlson was a snowboarder, not a skier, and a regular at Stevens Pass. Earlier that week, he competed at Washington's Crystal Mountain. Jack worked the event, and Carlson slept several nights in Jack's camper.

When Carlson and Pankey arrived at Stevens Pass that Sunday, they joined Tim Wesley, known to most as Tall Tim—a lanky 39-year-old snowboarder from Leavenworth. The three merged with those waiting for Rudolph.

Another arrival was Wenzel Peikert, 29, an off-duty Stevens Pass ski instructor from Seattle. Skiing over the weekend without his wife and infant daughter, he hung around the Foggy Goggle and the R.V. lot on Saturday night. He, too, sent a message to Rudolph on Sunday, confirming the plan.

"I wrote, 'Gear up?' " Peikert said. "And he wrote, 'Yeah, for sure.' So I went into the ski school and grabbed my pack, with my beacon, probe and shovel. I went to the fire pit and I met the whole group. You could tell they were a different level of skier by how they acted and how they dressed."

Among the strangers he saw was Rob Castillo, a 40-year-old father of two and former competitive skier. He had exchanged text messages with Jack.

Castillo and Jack lived together in Alta, Utah, for several years in the 1990s. They went helicopter skiing in Alaska and skied down mountains they had climbed in Washington.

"Tunnel Creek at 11," Jack wrote.

"Perfect," Castillo thought. "That's just what I wanted to do."

At the fire pit, Castillo considered the others.

"It was kind of like, 'All right, this group is getting bigger,' " Castillo said. "I wouldn't pop in with a bunch of no-names, necessarily, and trust any of them, but the ones I knew were definitely qualified to go. And they're not going to bring people out who aren't."

More than anything, Castillo wanted to ski for the first time all season with his two best friends at Stevens Pass—Jack and Johnny Brenan.

In the R.V. parking lot, a few hundred yards away, Johnny and Laurie Brenan convened in their motor home for an early lunch with their daughters, Josie, 10, and Nina, 7, part of the Stevens Pass ski teams.

Brenan, 41, grew up comfortably in the Seattle suburbs, not far from Jack. He followed his passion for skiing to Breckenridge, Colorado, working as a ski patroller in the winter and a carpenter in the summer. A burly man whose five o'clock shadow arrived by noon each day, he eventually opened a business that he named for home: Cascade Contracting.

"I met Johnny at the Gold Pan in Breckenridge," Laurie Brenan said. "It was Thursday night, 25-cent beer night. He was sitting on the pool table, and he had an open spot next to him. And I said, 'I'm going to go sit next to that cute guy.' "

They married in 1997 and moved to Leavenworth. Brenan worked as a cabinetmaker, then resurrected Cascade Contracting. On the strength of Brenan's amicable personality and no-fear creativity, it blossomed with custom homes and expansive remodels.

The Brenans bought a deteriorated 100-year-old farmhouse on a hill in an apple orchard. Johnny Brenan lifted the structure on jacks, rebuilt the foundation and gutted the inside, intending to resell it as a bed-and-breakfast. The Brenans kept it for themselves to raise their family.

Brenan zipped from one construction site to another in his truck. He coached soccer teams. He held Monday night poker games in the garage, which Nina always helped prepare. He built a chicken coop in the yard.

"Johnny and Josie bought five chickens, and they called the business Eggs, Ink," Laurie Brenan said. "They had signs and business cards. Then they bought 30 more chickens. It's like, she's 5 years old. But the more the merrier for Johnny, even with chickens."

Sunday began perfectly for Brenan. The family R.V. was parked in space No. 3, where the satellite dish picked up the best television reception. Brenan was at the front of the lift line at dawn.

He offered to fetch coffee for those behind him, a trick he used to keep his place while he helped Laurie get their daughters fed and dressed. He returned to the line, excited for an increasingly rare chance to ski with old friends like Jack.

"I dropped the kids off for ski team about 8:45," Laurie Brenan said. "I remember looking down and Johnny was yelling at Jim Jack, doing something with his hands, something crazy. They were like little boys in a candy store. They were so excited."

Back with his family for lunch, Brenan ate an egg sandwich and discussed a business deal on the phone. It was after 11, and he was afraid he would miss the Tunnel Creek run.

But Rudolph sent a couple of people text messages at about 11:15. He apologized for running late, and said he would be out in about 10 minutes.

Brenan had time. He made a pact with Josie.

"Josie, be ready at 2," Brenan said. "I'm going to come back and we'll go on a powder mission. Be here, because I'll be here."

Brenan strapped on his avalanche beacon, also called a transceiver, a device that emits a silent signal for others to detect your location in case of burial. A friend in the R.V. noted that its batteries were dead. Brenan replaced them with fresh ones.

"What's that, Papa?" Nina asked her father.

Brenan paused to show her how it worked.

"He explained it," Laurie Brenan said. "It was understood that avalanche beacons were really for body recovery. Not many people survive avalanches. He would say that."

Brenan gathered his things and headed toward the fire pit to join his friends.

"I said, 'Are you sure it's safe?'" Laurie Brenan said. "He looked me right in the eye and said: 'Of course. I wouldn't be going if it weren't.' I said O.K. because I knew that was true."

At about 11:30, Rudolph burst through the doors of the lodge at Stevens Pass. He was surprised by the size of the group waiting for him, but he barely broke stride.

"Get me out of here before another spreadsheet finds me," he said.

The group, jolted into action, scattered to gather gear.

"We all rallied up, jumped on the lifts," Castillo said. "I remember seeing some other buddies of mine later, like: 'Oh, I wanted to go out so bad with you guys that day. It looked like such a fun crew.'"

THE BACKCOUNTRY BECKONS

Stevens Pass opened in the winter of 1937–38 with a rope tow on Big Chief Mountain. A lodge and five new tows were added in the 1940s, including a mile-long T-bar that pulled people up the side of Cowboy Mountain. The ski area took shape in the bowl below the crescent-shape ridge that connects the two mountains.

Seventh Heaven, a two-person lift up a steep wall of Cowboy Mountain, changed the complexion of Stevens Pass when it was built in 1960. It opened a high swath of expert terrain, now marked as double diamond—experts only—on posted signs and the ski map.

It also provided easy access to the top of the high ridgeline. Back then, few people dared to remove their skis and hike the few hundred extra feet to the summit. "When I was younger at Stevens, no one skied off Cowboy —maybe just a few locals," said Wangen, who has skied the area for nearly five decades. "But the last 20 years, it's gone ballistic."

Now there is a steady procession of expert skiers and snowboarders through the boundary gate next to the top of the lift. Most drop off the left side of the ridge, back into the resort, through the rocky and narrow chutes.

Those who drop away from the ski area, toward Tunnel Creek, are simply following a much wider trend into "sidecountry"—backcountry slopes easily entered by lifts and, sometimes, a short hike.

"I don't like the term 'sidecountry,'" Moore, the avalanche forecaster, said. "It makes it sound like 'backcountry light.'"

The rise of backcountry skiing can be credited to a collision of factors.

Ski areas that once vigilantly policed their boundaries, from Jackson Hole, Wyoming, to Squaw Valley, California, have gradually opened their gates to the territory surrounding them. While that has led to wrangling over liability issues and raised debate over search-and-rescue responsibilities, most areas note that they are carved out of public land. They really cannot keep people from going there.

But ski areas also see the potential to attract more ticket-buying customers, and more influential ones, by blurring the boundary lines. Many areas slyly promote not just the terrain inside their borders, but the wilder topography beyond, using the power of media and word of mouth —as Rudolph did for Stevens Pass.

Skiing adjacent to ski areas, however, can numb people to risk. Easy access, familiar terrain and a belief that help is just a short distance away may lead people to descend slopes they might avoid in deeper wilderness.

While most backcountry users would not consider entering known avalanche territory without a beacon, one study last winter at Loveland Ski Area in Colorado found that fewer than 40 percent of people who passed through a boundary gate wore one.

Equipment advances have emboldened people. Intermediate powder skiers have been turned into expert ones thanks to fatter skis and the "rocker" shape of their tips—design advances borrowed from snowboarding. Popular ski bindings now temporarily detach at the heel, allowing skiers to glide up rises like a cross-country skier, then reconnect so they can descend like a professional downhiller.

Snowboards have borrowed from skis, too. Some models can be quickly split into two pieces, allowing users to stride up short hills in pursuit of bigger descents.

Similar advances in safety gear, like easy-to-use digital beacons and air bags, have helped make the backcountry feel less dangerous. Beacons help rescuers find people buried under the snow, while air bags deploy a large balloon meant to help keep the skier closer to the surface of an avalanche. A leading American manufacturer of safety gear is named, appropriately, Backcountry Access.

Companies, including Salomon and Flylow, have marketed heavily to ride the backcountry trend. They are keenly aware that many buyers will never ski the backcountry but want to dress the part.

Those marketing shifts have coincided with a generation raised on the glorification of risk. From X Games to YouTube videos, helmet cameras to social media, the culture rewards vicarious thrills and video one-upmanship. This generation no longer automatically adheres to the axiom of waiting a day for safer conditions. The relative placidness of inbounds skiing is no match for the greater adventure of untamed terrain.

Among avalanche forecasters and the growing cottage industry of safety instructors, there is pride in noting that the number of fatalities has risen at a slower rate than the number of backcountry users. But they see themselves as part of a difficult race between the coming hordes and the tools to protect them.

"You could argue that skiers have never been this educated or safe," Stifter, the *Powder* magazine editor, said. "There's been a huge emergence and emphasis on avalanche classes. Then you also have this lifesaving technology. But if you go to Jackson or Utah, you'll see people who are not educated, who are just going out there because they see it in the movies and they see it in magazines like *Powder*: there's fresh tracks and, man, it looks like fun."

At the top of Seventh Heaven, the members of the group took off their skis and snowboards. Directly to the right of the lift's unloading ramp was a narrow trail that disappeared up through a clog of trees.

"Read this," one sign read in all capital letters. "Ski Area Boundary. Minimum of $1000.00 rescue fee! Do you have a partner, beacon, probe and shovel? Explosives may be used in this area at any time. Continue at your own risk."

A smaller sign read: "Stop. Ski Area Boundary. No ski patrol or snow control beyond this point."

To the right was a small gray steel box. It was labeled, "Avalanche Transceiver Check Station."

"You walk by and it goes beep, beep," Rob Castillo said. "So as we were going through, you heard it going all the way, right on everyone. Beep. Beep. Beep."

While there are no laws dictating what equipment people carry into the backcountry, there is a code. Carry a beacon (for sending and receiving signals), a probe (for poking for victims in the snow) and a shovel (for digging them out).

"When you go in the backcountry, you're trusting your life in the hands of everybody else and they're trusting their life in you," Michelson said. "If I get buried and my ski partner doesn't have a beacon, shovel or probe, it's my life on the line."

One member of the party did not elicit a beep: Erin Dessert, a 35-year-old snowboarder who was early for her afternoon shift as a Stevens Pass lift operator. Wesley invited her along. She thought everyone was riding off the front side of Cowboy Mountain, back into the ski area.

The group marched single file along the narrow ridge for a few minutes until it reached a wider area to convene. Tracks dropped back over a steep edge and into the ski area to the left.

To the right was nothing but deep powder, hidden by thick trees, like a curtain to the big attraction.

THE DESCENT BEGINS

There were 16 people, although no one thought to count at the time. Their ages ranged from 29 to 53.

"This was a crew that seemed like it was assembled by some higher force," Dessert said.

It was about 11:45. The storm had passed. A low, pewter sky hid the surrounding peaks. Castillo glanced around at the others, wearing helmets and rainbow hues, a kaleidoscope of color amid the gray surroundings, like sprinkles on vanilla ice cream.

"I was thinking, wow, what a bunch of heavies," he said.

There was loose banter and a few casual introductions. Not everyone met everyone else. Someone pulled out marijuana to smoke, and passed it.

Wesley, the snowboarder known as Tall Tim, saw the size of the assembled group. More than a dozen, he thought.

"That never happens," he said. "And it's basically the legends of Stevens Pass standing up there."

There was little doubt that those with Tunnel Creek experience knew the way. About half the group had been down dozens of times each, if not hundreds. The others would follow.

There was no broad discussion of the route down. Pockets of the group talked about staying left, not being too greedy by going too far down the meadow before cutting across.

"That run, it's not that it's supersteep, or there are cliffs, or that it's a really rowdy run," Carlson, one of the Stevens Pass regulars, said. "It's that if anything goes wrong, it's a terrain trap. If somebody happens to set off even a slough slide and you're below them in Tunnel, it all bottlenecks and really adds up superfast. That's the reason that run is heavy. It's notorious."

Unspoken anxiety spread among those unfamiliar with the descent. The mere size of the group spooked some. Backcountry users of all types —skiers, snowboarders, snowmobilers and climbers—worry about how much of a load a slope can absorb before it gives way. They worry about people above them causing an avalanche. When it comes to the back-country, there is usually not safety in large numbers.

That is not only because of the physical impact on the snow. It is because of the complicated dynamics that large groups create. Deadly avalanches are usually the product of bad decisions—human nature, not Mother Nature.

"If it was up to me, I would never have gone backcountry skiing with 12 people," Michelson, the ESPN journalist, said. "That's just way too many. But there were sort of the social dynamics of that—where I didn't want to be the one to say, you know, 'Hey, this is too big a group and we shouldn't be doing this.' I was invited by someone else, so I didn't want to stand up and cause a fuss. And not to play the gender card, but there were 2 girls and 10 guys, and I didn't want to be the whiny female figure, you know? So I just followed along."

Others suppressed reservations, too.

"The whole thing felt rushed to me, and it felt kind of like this covert operation," Stifter said. "Which it kind of was, because you're going out of bounds. It's obviously acceptable, especially when you're going out there with all these locals and the director of marketing. It's not illegal or anything. It just had this rushed feeling from the time Chris walked out of the office, and he's like, 'All right, let's go.' "

Carlsen, Stifter's *Powder* colleague, was uneasy. He tried to convince himself that it was a good idea.

"There's no way this entire group can make a decision that isn't smart," he said to himself. "Of course it's fine, if we're all going. It's got to be fine."

After a few minutes, the small talk faded. Worries went unexpressed.

"When you're up on top of a peak like that, it's usually hang out for a second, and then it's momentum," Castillo said. "You just kind of feel it. Everyone's like: 'O.K., we're not here to hang out. Let's start going.' So I saw people starting to slide, get going, and I was like: 'Hey, Johnny, partner up. Buddy system. Let's go. Me and you.' And at that point, it clicked. Everyone's like, yeah, partners, partners, partners."

It is a tenet of avalanche safety, and the command snapped the group to attention.

"Someone said, 'Partner up—everyone should grab a partner,'" Carlsen said. "Immediately I thought, We're in a somewhat serious situation. It wasn't just grab a partner so you don't get lost. It was grab a partner so you. ...

"It just felt bigger all of a sudden."

Rudolph, the Stevens Pass marketing director, teamed with Saugstad, the professional skier.

"I was really excited about that," Saugstad said, "because he's just such a cool guy and I thought, wow, cool, he wants to be my partner. A very trustworthy guy that's an amazing skier."

Jack, on borrowed Salomon skis, paired with Joel Hammond, the Salomon representative. Carlson looked at Pankey, his childhood friend.

"Dude, you're coming with me," he said.

Wesley gave a little whistle to Carlson and Pankey and nodded downhill. He wanted to be first. The conditions were too good to waste time, and he did not want to be slowed by the huge pack.

With little warning, Wesley dropped straight through the large cluster of trees, using firs as a slalom course. Pankey and Carlson followed.

Rudolph, always up for competition, sped around the trees, not through them. He curved around a banked C-shape turn that dropped him a couple hundred feet into the broad meadow below.

He arrived just in time to see Wesley, Pankey and Carlson burst from the trees into the open powder. Rudolph pointed his ski poles and playfully shouted invectives as their tracks crossed.

Wesley laughed, and his two friends followed him left and over a small rise.

Rudolph headed straight down the mountain.

"I remember looking back at where he was going and being confused," Wesley said. "Like, 'Where is he going?' "

All the locals in the group presumed they knew what the others were thinking. They did not.

"When you know an avalanche is not very likely, that's a great way to go," Wesley said of Rudolph's choice to ski straight down farther. "It's three open glades of awesome powder."

Earlier that morning, Wesley and Carlson had skied the opposite side of Cowboy Mountain, in the ski area. It had been cleared of avalanches by the ski patrol at dawn, but the two still triggered several slough slides— small, shallow avalanches that washed at their feet and petered out before snagging victims.

"That's why, when they said we're doing Tunnel, I was like, 'Ooh, dicey,'" Wesley said.

Pankey and Carlson followed Wesley and looked back, too, wondering why Rudolph and the others were not following them toward relatively safer terrain. Within a minute, long enough to be well out of sight of the group they left behind, the three men found something that made them stop.

"We were right on top of a knoll, a little rollover, where we were about to make some really fun turns, and we saw that the face had already slid," Carlson said. "It was pretty large."

Alarmed, the three decided to go farther left. They crossed through trees and avoided big meadows and steep pitches. They soon found evidence of another avalanche, this one cutting through the forest.

"I'd really never seen anything slide in the trees like that," Carlson said. "And that was definitely like: 'Holy cow, we shouldn't be back here, Ron. Let's go left. Let's go hard left.'"

Wesley had disappeared in the pale light. He left nothing but a track through the deep snow that the others tried to follow.

"I just went, and didn't really stop," Wesley said. "I went all the way down. But I've never taken a run where I looked uphill more times in fear."

"I GOT EYES ON YOU"

Rudolph stopped on the left edge of the upper meadow, above a cluster of trees. Others filed behind him, spilling down the mountain in plumes of spraying snow.

Erin Dessert did not follow. She was confused. She was once a Tunnel Creek regular, until a nonfatal avalanche captured five friends in 2002 and scared her away.

"Chris Rudolph's, like, totally all about safety protocol and mountain awareness and wisdom," she said. "That guy knows the conditions like an animal. He has instincts. It didn't register, even for a second, that he might be bringing this group to Tunnel Creek. It wasn't logical. I thought we were doing the front side."

She headed hard to the right, away from the others. The other snowboarders that she knew, Carlson and Wesley, were gone in the opposite direction. Some in the remaining group noticed Dessert heading away in the distance and dismissed her as an oblivious backcountry rookie. She dipped out of sight in a lonely panic.

"I've been riding Stevens Pass since I was 3 years old," Dessert said. "I can tell circumstances, and I just felt like something besides myself was in charge. They're all so professional and intelligent and driven and powerful and riding with athletic prowess, yet everything in my mind was going off, wanting to tell them to stop."

Rudolph and the others, now a group of 12, were focused downhill. It was 11:52 a.m. Rudolph did not wait for the back of the pack to arrive before continuing to demonstrate the way.

"So Chris Rudolph went first, and then he pulled into the trees and we waited for a sec," said Castillo, who was near the front of the group, wearing a helmet camera. "He goes out of sight and behind the trees. So I said, 'O.K., Megan, go ahead, spoon those tracks, and you'll see Chris on the left.' "

It was not Megan Michelson. It was Elyse Saugstad.

"I thought it was Megan," Castillo said. "I said, 'Are you Megan?' She said, 'No, no, I'm Elyse.' That's when I met Elyse. It was right there. And she made these turns that were like: 'Aah, I think I know who that is. I've seen her name. Those are pro turns.' She ripped the hell out of it."

She traced through the knee-deep snow just to the right of Rudolph's elongated S-shape tracks. She dipped through trees at a pinch in the meadow and disappeared out of sight. She crossed over Rudolph's tracks and giggled. After about 30 seconds, she was back at Rudolph's side, having cut left into a notch of the trees again.

"We skied to an area that was probably about 500 feet down or so from where we started," Saugstad said. "And where we skied to was an area of old-growth trees. You know, several-hundred-year-old trees. A very good indication that this is a safe place. Things don't happen here."

Castillo and Brenan teased each other about who would go next.

"Finally, he's like, 'Go ahead, I got eyes on you,' " Castillo said.

From where Rudolph and Saugstad stopped, they could not see the subsequent skiers approach. Castillo went past and cut left. His camera recorded Rudolph and Saugstad whooping their approval as he stopped in a shower of powder, about 40 feet below them.

But just before he stopped, Castillo was jolted by a weird sensation.

"A little pang, like, ooh, this is a pretty heavy day out here," Castillo said. "Thing's holding, but I remember having a feeling."

Castillo stopped above two trees. He nestled close and pushed his right ski tight against them.

"A lot of people think you should be below trees, but I stand above them," Castillo said. "I'm like, 'I'd rather get pinned against this than taken through.' "

His helmet camera showed that 14 seconds after Castillo stopped, Brenan appeared through the trees above Rudolph and Saugstad. Brenan had hugged the tree line on the left, avoiding the open meadow, then slalomed through the patch that the others used for protection. He stopped in a spray of snow a few feet from Rudolph and Saugstad.

"That was sick!" someone shouted.

Castillo silently took note of the terrain.

"I was downhill from them—skier's right from them," Castillo said. "But the trees that they were behind, I didn't think it was a bad spot to stop. They were huge. Giant old-growths that three of us probably can't put our hands around."

But he knew the direction of the slope did not follow the meadow. It dipped harder left into the trees, down toward a gully. And there were still a lot of skiers above them.

Saugstad was next to Rudolph. Brenan was a few feet away.

"We weren't straight across from each other, in a perfect horizontal line on the slope," Saugstad said. "We were peppered up and down, spread out."

Castillo kept his attention up the hill. Less than 30 seconds after Brenan stopped, he saw Tim Wangen cut through the trees above the earlier arrivals, gliding horizontally through the forest. Wangen had been taught how to navigate Tunnel Creek by his father. He knew that the farther down the mountain he went, the harder it would be to cut over the ridge and into the next big meadow. He crossed the shallow gully and rose up the other side.

"I could see the others when I cut over," Wangen said. "I thought: Oh yeah, that's a bad place to be. That's a bad place to be with that many people. But I didn't say anything. I didn't want to be the jerk."

Wangen had told Peikert to follow his tracks, and Peikert was close behind. Castillo watched where they went.

"Want to cut over?" Castillo shouted to those above him.

SLIDING SNOW

The start of an avalanche is unlike any other force of nature.

A hurricane is foretold by wind and lashing waves. A tornado often is spotted before it strikes. Lightning is usually presaged by black clouds and rumbling thunder.

Avalanches rarely provide such a warning. Unlike waves or wind, tremors or storms, they are usually triggered by their own victims, sometimes unaware of what has been unleashed.

"If you swim out in the ocean, the ocean's always alive," Saugstad said. "You can feel it. But the mountains feel like they're asleep."

Back up the mountain, Jack never seemed worried. That was his nature. Here he was, a rare weekend off, skiing with some of his best friends from Leavenworth and people from Powder and ESPN and all over the industry, on an epic run on a perfect powder day.

Carlsen, the *Powder* photographer, had never been to Tunnel Creek. The first few easy turns gave way to a slope that fell steeply away, out of sight. He sidled up to Jack.

"I grabbed him, and I said, 'What is the move here?'" Carlsen said. "It was basically like, 'This is getting real, how do we handle it?' He's like: 'Oh, no big deal. We go out here, swing out, make a few pow turns, and get back in the trees.' I looked at him and said, 'Have a great run.' Gave him a fist, a knuckle-to-knuckle high-five thing. And that was it. I watched him swing out, way out, skier's right, and then dive into his turn left."

Jack flowed through the thick powder with his typical ease. He skied the way other people walked down a sidewalk, a friend had said.

Jack disappeared over the knoll, gliding through the trees in the middle of the meadow. Behind him, the five remaining skiers watched in silence.

"He looked like he was having a great time, the run of his life, in fact," Michelson said. "And he actually made, I remember, a little 'woo' sound, as he dropped in on his first or second turn because the snow was really good. It was deep and light."

Then the snow changed without warning.

Across the meadow, above Jack, loose snow seemed to chase him down the hill and out of sight.

Not everyone saw it. A couple did. They caught it in their peripheral vision and were unsure what to make of it.

"That was sketchy," Hammond said.

The five others listened. Not a sound. They stared for clues through the flat light below a murky sky. Nothing.

Silent seconds ticked. Finally, Hammond spotted the first sign of evidence. It came from a tree, one among thousands, far down the hill, almost out of sight. Only the top of it was visible, and it was covered in snow.

"I saw it moving," Hammond said. "Like something had hit the tree, and it shook. And I could see the powder falling off the tree."

BLUR OF WHITE

A few hundred yards down the mountain, a ghostly white fog rushed through the forest.

"I saw it," Saugstad said. "I saw it coming. But it was weird because it was coming through the trees. It was like snow billowing through the trees. Because it was such a treed area, I think for the first second I saw it I didn't believe it."

Wangen and Peikert had just traversed in front of its path. It did not miss them by much.

"I don't know if I'd even come to a stop when I heard it," Peikert said. "It was almost like wind and pressure more than noise. It literally felt like a freight train went over my tails. It wasn't a deep rumble. I could feel this rush of air."

It was a blur of white, its shattered pieces moving about 50 m.p.h., a powder cloud two stories tall.

Rudolph was the only one to scream.

"Avalanche! Elyse!" Rudolph shouted.

Saugstad tried to stride right, hoping to escape. She barely moved before snow flowed through her legs, dragging her down like a riptide.

She pulled the cord on her air bag. She was overwhelmed so quickly by the rising snow that she did not know if it inflated.

"I had no ability to control what was happening to me," Saugstad said. "I was being tossed over and over and over. It was like being in a washing machine and all my body parts flailing every way. I didn't know which way was up. I didn't know which way was down. I couldn't see anything."

She is likely to have tumbled just past Castillo. He groaned and turned his face away. He stuck his head between two trees, like a prisoner in a stockade.

For 16 seconds, snow and ice pounded his back and washed over him. His shoulders were jammed against the trees. His face pushed into branches of pine needles. He could feel the barrage of snow lashing at his back.

Trees cracked around him. Some in the path were chopped in half — the stumps left in the soil, the rest carried away in the growing torrent.

The avalanche, a relatively small one, started with about 6,000 cubic meters of snow and collected 7,000 cubic meters more on the way down. It probably weighed about 11 million pounds.

The trees Castillo hugged in each arm swayed but held. He told himself that when he felt the flow slow, he would pop a hand in the air so that it might stick out of the snow and make him easier to rescue.

"Just as I had the thought about what I'm going to do, wondering if it was going to bury me, that's right when I could feel it," Castillo said. "It was like a wave. Like when you're in the ocean and the tide moves away from you. You're getting thrashed and you feel it pull out and you're like, O.K., I can stand up now."

Castillo saw daylight again. His camera captured snow sliding past his legs for another 13 seconds. The forest sounded as if it were full of sickly frogs. It was the trees, scrubbed of their fresh snow, still swaying and creaking around him.

Castillo turned to look back up the hill.

"Where there were three people, there was nobody," Castillo said.

A TICKING CLOCK

He did not know who or what set off the avalanche. He did not know how far down the mountain it went. All he knew was that about a dozen people had been above him a minute earlier, and that the gully below him descended another 2,000 vertical feet to the valley floor.

And he was alone.

"Johnny! Johnny Brenan!" Castillo screamed into the stillness, his voice escalating with panic. The scope of the disaster was too much to comprehend. He wanted to find his partner.

"So I'm screaming his name," Castillo said. "I'm screaming and screaming. Silence."

Streams of snow still flowed downhill as he scooted toward the heart of the slide path. It flowed into a wide gully, maybe 100 feet across, that narrowed as it descended. Castillo turned his beacon to "search" mode, meaning he would receive signals of those buried, but would not emit signals himself.

"I don't want to be in this gully because I don't know what's coming down next," Castillo said. "I don't want to be the next guy taken out. Now I don't even have a beacon on because I'm on search. They're not going to find me if anything happens to me."

Across the gully, unable to see anyone else, either, Peikert and Wangen had gone into search mode, too.

"I was like, if there's someone in that, the clock's ticking," Peikert said.

Chances of survival drop precipitously every minute. According to a recent study, the survival rate for individuals completely buried in an avalanche falls to about 40 percent after 15 minutes of burial and to 25 percent after 30 minutes. About 75 percent of avalanche victims die from asphyxia or suffocation. The other 25 percent of fatalities result from trauma.

Castillo spotted Peikert and Wangen across the gully. They, too, were nervous about hangfire, the unstable snow left along the edges of an avalanche's path that can release at any moment.

The avalanche had turned the gully into an oversize bobsled run, with slick, high-banked walls.

"This gully's hard-core!" Castillo yelled. "They're in it!"

Wangen stayed mostly on the banks. Peikert and Castillo crossed the gully a couple of times, reluctantly and quickly.

"What's your name again?" Castillo shouted at Peikert.

It was soon apparent that the victims, however many there were, suffered one of two fates: they were hung up on the banks of the gully, snagged by a tree or buried in snow, or they had been flushed to the bottom, thousands of feet below.

If searchers spent too much time looking along the gully, they might squander a chance at rescuing someone at the bottom. If they rushed down-hill, they might pass someone in need of saving.

"We started to ski down, hoping to find him in a tree well or hanging on or something," said Castillo, his focus on Brenan. "But I started to realize all the trees were bent over, and I started thinking, this is really fricking bad. And then I skied down to a point where I found Johnny's ski, probably three or four feet up in a tree. Stuck."

Castillo called 911. It was 12:02 p.m. The avalanche occurred seven minutes earlier.

"Hi, I'm at Stevens Pass resort, on the backside of Tunnel Creek," Castillo told the King County Sheriff's Department dispatcher. He added, "We had a major avalanche, and we might have three or four people missing, at least."

The dispatcher asked him to slow down. Castillo, occasionally shouting at others nearby, tried to explain where the avalanche occurred. He was asked how many people there were.

"There's at least 10," Castillo said. "Between 10 and 12."

The dispatcher asked if anybody was hurt.

"We haven't found them," Castillo said. "I found one ski. It rolled through pretty heavy, man. I had partners right next to me and they're missing. I just found a ski about 1,000 yards down. Or 1,000 feet down."

The call lasted four minutes. Castillo, carrying his friend's ski, turned down the mountain.

"THIS THING RIPPED BIG"

Near the top, the five skiers who planned to follow Jim Jack deciphered what happened through a series of increasingly blunt clues. Loose snow. A shaking tree.

Hammond was due to ski next. He took a couple of turns through the fine powder of the meadow and stopped. There was a sudden drop, nearly three feet deep. The fluffy snow was gone. A surface of bluish ice stretched down the hill, into the trees and out of sight.

"Once I had gotten to the edge, I was like, oh my gosh, this thing ripped big," Hammond said. "I could see the scope of it."

He shouted for everyone to go into search mode. The other four skiers moved quickly to see.

"We all skied up to it and were like, holy smokes," Stifter said. "From there all I remember was pulling out my phone. And I called Jim Jack."

Others started dialing numbers, too. They called Chris Rudolph and Elyse Saugstad. There were no answers. Hammond dropped onto the slick slide path. Another clue lay on the ice, pointing downhill.

"I hopped out there and made one or two turns, and I saw one of Jim's skis," Hammond said. "The only reason I recognized Jim's skis was that it was a pair of skis that he borrowed from me."

The realization that Jack had been carried away was a gut punch.

"In one respect, you're like, oh no, a ski—where's Jim?" Abrams said. "On the other hand, you think, O.K., there's his ski. Let's find him."

Michelson called 911. According to sheriff's department records, it was 12:03 p.m.

Her voice was steady and sure. She patiently tried to explain where they were—"The backside of the ski area in the backcountry," she explained. "Tunnel Creek."

The dispatcher asked if people were buried.

"I believe so, yes," Michelson replied. "I don't know how many. We have a large group."

Word was relayed to the ski area. Chris Brixey, manager of the Stevens Pass Ski Patrol, had 17 patrollers working on the mountain that day, two more in the aid room, and a dispatcher. Brixey is a regular at Johnny Brenan's Monday night poker parties. He did not know that a group of friends, including Rudolph, his Stevens Pass co-worker, had gone to Tunnel Creek.

"I happened to be walking through the aid room," Brixey said. "Our dispatcher handed me a note that said 10 people are buried in Tunnel Creek. I called the 911 operator and got Megan's information. I called Megan directly. She said there's about 12 people and they were looking for eight people. I didn't know Megan. My gut feeling was that this was a group of inexperienced people who are now dealing with tragedy."

Brixey called the area's most seasoned patroller and put him in charge of the four-member first-response unit, called the hasty team, to follow the group's trail. He also enlisted other patrollers and a pair of avalanche rescue dogs.

Word of a large avalanche in Tunnel Creek soon echoed around Stevens Pass, from the patrol room to the R.V. lot, up the lifts and down the slopes. According to the Stevens Pass Ski Patrol log, the area closed public access to the boundary gate atop the Seventh Heaven lift at 12:19.

By then, the group that had started off together less than 30 minutes earlier was strewn up and down nearly 3,000 vertical feet. No one knew how many were missing.

Keith Carlsen was nearest the top, searching for Jack.

"I thought someone has to make sure he's not still up here," Carlsen said. "It wasn't likely, but his ski was there, and he got swept, and there's no sign of him, so maybe he got pummeled into the snow, into a hole, somewhere, right away."

The others headed down, scanning the path and its edges with their beacons. Carlsen methodically checked the upper meadow.

"I thought I was going to be the one to find him, and I would find him alone," Carlsen said. "And the bed surface at the top was rock hard. And I'm thinking: I'm going to get a signal, and this guy's going to be buried, and I'm going to have to somehow dig him out. I'm going to find Jim Jack."

Scared and alone, Carlsen's voice broke the silence.

"I'm saying, and I remember repeating this in my head: 'Jim, am I about to find you? Jim, are you underneath me? Jim, where the hell are you? Is this possible? Is he really underneath here? Am I about to dig Jim out?' "

Farther down, others followed the path into the gully. As it descends toward the valley floor, it carves deeper into the mountain. In some spots, canyon walls are 20 feet high. There were steep, icy drops that would become gushing waterfalls during the spring runoff.

"There are places it's so tight that I would stop and my skis would straddle the middle," Hammond said. "And I'd be elevated, like being on springs."

It was still clogged with rocks and trees that had not been fully scoured away. Where the ravine bent, the avalanche rode high on the outside wall, like a child on a water slide, sometimes breaking over the top of the bank and unearthing trees on the ridges.

"It was fear," Abrams said. "Fear that you lost someone, and fear that you're standing in an avalanche path. You're thinking, Don't get caught up on trees, listen for the beacons, where's my fiancée?"

It became increasingly evident that whoever was caught in the avalanche would be found at the bottom.

"I probably went down for one or two minutes and I got no signal," Michelson said. "I shouted: 'They've gone all the way down! The way this gully is, they've been flushed.' "

DISCOVERY

Tim Carlson and Ron Pankey, having split from the big group at the top, nervously negotiated the roundabout route to the bottom of Tunnel Creek. They could not catch up to Tim Wesley, but followed his snowboard track to the valley floor. It was 12:07 p.m.

They glided past the foot of a mound of chunky debris. One of the ravines had spewed a sizable avalanche, but there was no way to know it had occurred in the past few minutes.

"I looked up and I saw a ski pole sticking up," Carlson said. "It looked like someone stuck it in there. It was sticking up right at the very end of the pile. Handle up."

He shouted to Pankey.

"I was like, 'Dude, you need to turn your transceiver on,' " Carlson said. " 'There's people in here.' "

Carlson clicked out of his snowboard bindings and climbed onto the pile. Pankey turned his beacon to search mode. It beeped immediately.

His skis off, Pankey climbed onto the debris pile, too. He saw the ski pole and two gloves. He was sucker-punched by dread.

"You figure someone who is fighting is going to have his gloves on," Pankey said. "If they're limp, yeah, their gloves are going to come off."

Then he noticed the brand.

"That was my thought—Oh, God, those are Scott gloves. Jim Jack was wearing Scott gloves," Pankey said.

Their beacons shrieked.

"I probably searched for maybe a minute before I was on top of a signal," Carlson said. "Your signal goes 'beepbeepbeepbeepbeepBEEP-BEEPBEEPBEEPBEEP,' and it gets a little fainter, like oh, over here. I got a strong signal, traversed over, got a weak signal, went back, got a strong signal, went back and I was basically on top of a body.

"And, uh, the first shovel I dug in, I hit Jim Jack's arm."

The two men dug frantically.

"I saw Jim Jack's face," Carlson said. "Eyes open, just staring at me. We could see he wasn't breathing. Ron started giving him breaths and I was searching for his body, underneath his chest. I was like, 'What the hell is going on?' There was no body where you'd expect a body to be. And then I started digging around, and I could see he was folded up into this ball. His feet were above his head."

His body had been pummeled.

"There was no blood, but he didn't have his helmet on, he didn't have his backpack on, his jacket was pulled over his head," Carlson said. "He had some scrapes on his belly. And just pulling him out of the snow you could feel it and see it. Giving him a couple of breaths, it just came out so quick. And you push on his chest and it would just collapse. There was nothing there. And Jim Jack—we're all strong dudes, and there was just nothing left."

"I pulled his arm upright, and it was just really soft," Carlson added. "It was like pulling a wet towel. Pulled the other arm and it was the same feeling. And I pulled his legs out, and there was nothing connected to anything. It was completely crushed."

They turned off Jack's beacon and tried to lay him peacefully in the snow. Pankey pushed his eyelids closed.

He called 911 at 12:31 p.m. and told the dispatcher that Jack was dead.

Jack's phone chirped. It had survived the avalanche, and Pankey reached into Jack's pocket and pulled it out. It was a text message from Jack's girlfriend, Tiffany Abraham. Rumors of a big avalanche in Tunnel Creek had reached the base area of Stevens Pass.

"Where are you?" it read. "You OK?"

Pankey looked over at the ski pole sticking straight out of the snow. It looked familiar. Pankey had noticed it on the hike up the ridge to Cowboy Mountain.

"That's the guy's in front of me," Pankey said. "He was hiking in front of me and Jim Jack was behind me, and he had these old Smith, corrective angle, curved poles. So I'm like, 'That's Johnny's pole.' "

"It Was Just a Bad Dream"

At the upper end of the meadow, more than 100 yards away and out of sight, Elyse Saugstad waited in the silence, unable to move.

She did not know how long she had been frozen there—head pointed downhill, hands sticking out of the snow, face poking through the ice just enough to breathe and to see the breaking clouds trailing the weekend's storm.

Her hip ached. Her mind wandered. She wondered who else was caught in the avalanche. She wondered who was left to rescue them.

She felt herself getting colder. Her pink mittens, like those of a child's, had strings that attached them to her jacket. When she had come to a stop, one of the mittens was on her hand. The other was off, hanging from her wrist.

Saugstad could not claw the hard-packed snow with her mittens on. She took them off and picked at the ice until her fingers ached. She put her mittens on again until they warmed up.

She had not spoken since the avalanche stopped. It had not occurred to her to cry for help. Someone would come. She hoped.

Finally, for the first time, she shouted.

"Help!" she screamed.

The face of Wenzel Peikert startled her.

Among those who skied down the gully, Peikert arrived first to the avalanche's final resting place. The walls of the ravine slowly fell away and opened onto a wide, sloping meadow. It was covered by an enormous pile of chunky ice cubes, some fit for a cocktail glass, others the size of couches. The debris was filled with dirt, rocks and shredded tree parts.

It stretched about 150 yards down what remained of the slope. It was 10 or 20 feet tall, obstructing Peikert's view to the bottom. Peikert's beacon began its frantic chirping.

"I started getting a signal," Peikert said. "I marked it with one of my poles. That's what they teach, to mark where you start picking up a signal and keep working to where it gets stronger. I took my skis off because it was so hard to ski on that stuff. And as I got close to that signal, I saw two pink gloves sticking out."

Saugstad was about 20 feet downhill.

"Her feet were into the snow and her head was downhill, but I saw two pink gloves and her face," Peikert said. "I don't know if she uncovered her face or not, but it was just barely sticking out of the snow. And a little bit of orange from her backpack. I started digging her out, trying not to hurt her. I said, 'Are you O.K.?' And she said: 'I think so. My leg's kind of hurt.'"

Peikert pulled his shovel from his backpack and started to dig.

"For a pause, really quickly, I thought to myself: she's alive, she's breathing, her face is out of the snow," Peikert said. "I thought, let's go find others. But then I realized that more snow could come down. I found someone alive, and I needed to get her out of here."

Saugstad sensed his urgency.

"When he started unburying me, he flung his shovel and it went flying down the hill so far that he couldn't stop and go get it," she said. "And so then he had to start digging me out with his hands."

Peikert hurried, knowing that others were likely buried nearby.

"She was actually really hard to get out," he said. "One of her skis had stayed on, so it had kind of locked her into the snow. Even a ski boot gets locked in. I dug to get her ski off. It probably took five minutes of digging to get her out."

Finally, Michelson and Abrams arrived from above. They found Peikert and Saugstad on their feet.

"It didn't dawn on me that she had been buried," Michelson said. "I was relieved she was alive."

Over several minutes, others trickled down from above.

"Once we got to the bottom, when we got through the ravine and got to the mouth, I just remember saying, 'Oh, my God,' " Stifter said. "Snow chunks the size of boulders. That's when I realized the magnitude of everything. It looked like a war zone. It was chaos."

Michelson took charge as an impromptu site commander. No one was sure who was missing or how many victims there might be. Michelson used her beacon and pinpointed two spots for others to search, then continued sweeping the meadow to search for more.

"My numbers and directions were bouncing all over the place," Peikert said. "But Megan comes up and hers was right on it. Mine is a little bit older, but I don't know why it was bouncing around. I started probing, and I hit a spot where there obviously was something other than snow."

Peikert and Rob Castillo dug through the ice. It had been more than 30 minutes since the avalanche.

Johnny Brenan was discovered about three feet below the surface. He had been buried a few feet from Saugstad all along.

"I found his back first," Peikert said. "His head was really bent under. I tried to dig a hole through his armpit, to his head, thinking I might be able to get his face turned to give him C.P.R. There was blood. His chin was split open. His helmet was pushed back onto the back of his head and was filled with snow. One leg was off in a weird position, like he had a broken femur or hip or something. I finally got him out. He was cold. Blue."

Castillo, Brenan's longtime friend and ski partner, worked side by side with Peikert, at last getting his legs out.

"The muscles were just beat," Castillo said.

About 20 feet up the hill, Abrams, Wangen and Stifter zeroed in on a victim, too. It was the spot that Peikert had marked with his pole before he spotted Saugstad.

"We were still searching for the lowest signal," Stifter said. "And the lowest signal I got on the transceiver was 2.4, and it took me, like, half a second to realize, oh, that's six feet down because it's in meters. So I'm like, all right, this is our lowest reading. And I think on our third probe we struck something. I told Dan and Tim, 'All right, get the shovels out,' and we started digging."

Digging was nothing like scooping snowfall from a driveway. It was more like shoveling the chunky piles that snowplows leave along the side of a cleared highway, full of large pieces seemingly glued together.

"They're big mounds of snow and they're like concrete," Stifter said. "So you dig and dig, and then that person would rotate to the back and take a break and the guy who was second would start clearing snow out for the guy who is digging."

Quickly exhausted, they rotated frequently.

"It was just a bad dream," Abrams said. "I was standing there holding my shovel that I never intended to use, except maybe to get my car out."

Finally, they reached a victim: Chris Rudolph.

"He was lying facedown, so it was hard to get to his face," Stifter said. "And it was hard because we couldn't move him because he was just encased in there. His feet were buried really deeply. Finally I was able to get to his face. His face was blue. And so finally I was like: 'We've got to get his feet out! We've got to get his feet out!' That took another good couple of minutes to get his feet free. Then we gently pulled him out by his backpack."

Stifter performed C.P.R. on Rudolph: 2 breaths, 30 compressions, to the point of exhaustion.

Saugstad called 911. It was 12:40 p.m.

"I'm reporting an avalanche," she said, breathlessly.

Frantic voices behind her shouted encouragement.

"Come on! You can do it! Come on, buddy! Take a breath!"

The dispatcher said there were "units on scene." Saugstad said they had not arrived and asked if they were coming by helicopter.

"Uh, we do not have a helicopter yet in the area because of the avalanche risk," the dispatcher said.

Hammond was the last to arrive from above and took over trying to revive Rudolph.

"I definitely believed that there was a chance," Stifter said. "My hope dissipated certainly after Joel got there and I was sitting there. We knew. We looked at each other."

Twenty feet downhill, the huddle around Brenan slowly came to the same conclusion. Peikert had been performing C.P.R. for close to 30 minutes, with Castillo's help.

"I was hoping for a miracle then," Castillo said. "But I really kind of understood that he was probably dead."

An hour's worth of adrenaline dissolved to disheartened shock. A few other skiers had happened upon the scene, but no rescue help had arrived.

Saugstad walked around dazed, wearing her deflated air bag "like dead angel wings," Carlsen said. Castillo made his way to the bottom of the hill to learn that Jim Jack was dead, too. Erin Dessert, the snowboarder who had veered away from the group at the top, frightened by the direction everyone was headed, had cautiously made her way down and rediscovered the group. She cradled Rudolph's head as others tried their last attempts to resuscitate him.

"It's Chris Rudolph," she said. "You know? He's the knight in shining armor of Stevens Pass."

WORD SPREADS

Laurie Brenan and Tiffany Abraham, Jack's girlfriend, were both in the Bull's Tooth Pub and Eatery, on the second level of the Granite Peaks Lodge.

"I saw Tiffany sitting at the bar, and I sat a few seats away," Brenan said. "She says, 'I haven't seen Jim yet.' And I said, 'Oh, he and Johnny did Tunnel Creek.' "

The man next to Abraham, a neighbor from Leavenworth, overheard. There was an avalanche in Tunnel Creek, he said. Someone came into the restaurant a while ago and asked for volunteers to help search.

Abraham's heart sank. Normally a font of buoyant optimism, she had a sudden pang of dread.

"I downed my cocktail because I knew I'd need it," Abraham said. "The bartender was telling a story, and I was trying to be polite and listen, but I knew I had to get out of there. I got my lunch boxed up and walked down to the ski patrol office. I took the elevator, and it was the slowest elevator in the world."

She could tell immediately that bad news was waiting. She spotted a friend who was on his way to the scene.

"He grabs my hand and I screamed at him," Abraham said. "'What the hell is going on?'"

They went into the ski patrol room, on the ground level on the backside of the lodge. Inside is a first-aid room with beds for injured skiers. Beyond is a ski patrol break room, a couch against one wall.

Anne Hessburg, Rudolph's girlfriend, was sitting there, balled up in tears. She had skied all morning with a friend and taken an early lunch at the Iron Goat pizzeria. She walked up to the slope-side cabin that Rudolph had provided to the journalists from *Powder* magazine. Hessburg stored skis there. A friend received a call while she was there.

"Someone told him there was an avalanche in Tunnel Creek," Hessburg said. "He told me, and my stomach immediately dropped."

Hessburg rushed to the ski patrol room. She could tell by the way people were moving that it was something serious. She could hear the squawks on the walkie-talkies. Someone told her only that Rudolph was probably involved, as if to break the emotional fall.

Brixey, the ski patrol manager, confirmed it. Rudolph was dead. That was about when Abraham walked into the patrol room with her friend, noticing a broken Hessburg on the couch.

Abraham's friend turned to her, looked her in the eyes, and told her about Jack.

"Baby girl, he's gone," he said.

"I just lost my breath," Abraham said. "I lost it. I couldn't even be in my skin."

Laurie Brenan had no premonition. She watched Abraham rush out of the restaurant at the news of an avalanche and casually followed a few minutes behind.

"I thought everything was fine," she said. "But I'm going over to ski patrol. I felt like Johnny was probably using his skills, digging somebody out."

She tried to stay out of the way as people hurried in and out of the patrol room.

"Then I heard someone say something about Jim Jack, and I thought, oh my God, how can that be?" Brenan said. "I knew they were all in the same group. I start calling to see if I can get someone to get my kids safe, back to the R.V., and get them a snack and put on a movie or something."

Brenan spotted Brixey, the patrol manager and Monday night poker player, and waited for an opening to approach.

"I said, 'So, Chris, there's been an avalanche in Tunnel Creek?'" Brenan said. "And he said yes. Anyone hurt? He said yes. Is anyone dead? He said yes. And I said, 'Do I know these people?' And he said yes. I said, 'Where's Johnny?' And he said, 'I haven't heard.'"

It was true. One 911 call from Tunnel Creek had reported the death of Jack. Another had reported the death of Rudolph. A third made mention of a third fatality, but the dispatcher never asked the name. Brixey did not learn about Brenan until his own patrol members reached the scene.

"I went outside, totally shaking," Laurie Brenan said. "I kept dropping my water bottle, again and again, because I was shaking so much. Then Chris Brixey comes and gets me."

Brixey's outward calm belied the turmoil inside. As a paramedic, he had told a lot of strangers that a loved one had died. But never a close friend.

"That was, by far, the biggest challenge for me, walking Laurie from outside back to my office," Brixey said. "Not knowing what I was going to say, but knowing what I had to say."

They walked past the empty beds, past Hessburg on the couch, past Abraham. In the office, he turned to her.

"He said Johnny was one of the people buried," Brenan said. "'He didn't make it.' I didn't want to believe it. I said, 'Have you seen him?' He said no. I said: 'Then you don't know. It's possible he's not there. You go back and get more information because that is wrong. Go. Go find him. You're wrong.' I remember thinking: He's got two kids. This was for fun. Johnny doesn't leave his responsibilities. Ever."

Brixey left. Brenan melted into shock. Finally, a friend from Leavenworth came in. He had gone to ski Tunnel Creek about 20 minutes behind the large group and happened upon the scene.

"He said, 'I can tell you it was him,'" Laurie Brenan said. " 'I gave him C.P.R. We tried.'

"It really felt like I had died then," Brenan said. "And that I was reborn into a nightmare."

A GRIM VIGIL

Back on the other side of Cowboy Mountain, and down a meadow that had been turned inside out, weary huddles surrounded three dead men.

Hope had surrendered. Rescues became grim vigils. The survivors did not know what to do other than wait. The bodies and faces of the victims were covered in jackets because it seemed the respectful thing to do. Survivors introduced themselves to those they had not met.

A group of 16 skiers and snowboarders, all of them experts, all of them unable to refuse the temptation of an hourlong excursion into steep powder, had been reduced by three lives.

"I'm so done with it," Stifter thought to himself. "I'm so done with skiing."

The first ski patrollers, along with an avalanche dog named Cava, arrived at 1:05 p.m., 70 minutes after the mountain gave way. They had started at the top and combed the entire path, following the funnel from the wide upper meadow through the flumelike ravine, searching for victims along the way. By the time they spit out of the mouth at the bottom, there was no rescue to be done.

The patrollers recognized faces in the huddles. They realized then that they had been searching for friends, not strangers. They stopped to find Rudolph and Brenan. Another patroller headed farther down to learn about Jack.

More patrollers began to arrive from below, on snowmobiles brought from the highway. A scene of quiet contemplation buzzed with activity and a second wave of despair.

"It just became this sea, getting merged into everybody else's shock," Dessert said. "When it was just us out there working on them, it seemed beautiful and spiritual, almost like an Indian burial ground."

The patrollers tried to revive the victims. It was useless.

A medical examiner determined that Jack's cause of death was "subdural and subarachnoid hemorrhage"—brain trauma. She also diagnosed a partially torn aorta; a broken neck, vertebrae, sternum and ribs;

and lacerations of the liver, spleen and pancreas. She described "blunt force injury of the head, neck, torso and extremities."

Rudolph, with a "blunt force injury of the torso," sustained "rib fractures with right hemothorax and probably compressional asphyxia." Brenan had "blunt force injury and compression of the trunk," with "multiple rib and vertebral fractures with probable compressional asphyxia."

They were probably dead by the time the avalanche stopped, or shortly after.

Brixey, working by radio over the mountain at Stevens Pass, told all rescue units to stand down. A second surge of patrollers would assist in taking the bodies off the mountain.

The survivors were encouraged to make their way to the highway, where ambulances awaited. Saugstad, missing a ski, used the one of Jack's that had been found. Hammond had been carrying it on his back.

Stifter and Carlsen sat on the meadow, unable to pull themselves away.

"Everybody kind of skied down," Stifter said. "It seemed weird to me to leave the bodies."

As with other survivors, the quarrel with their own guilt began immediately, the first sign that avalanches swallow more lives than just the ones buried beneath the snow.

They wondered if their mere presence at Stevens Pass that weekend gave rise to the Tunnel Creek trip, a group of proud locals eager to show off for influential out-of-towners. They wondered why they recognized all of the danger signs, starting with the avalanche report that morning over coffee, but did not do enough to slow or stop the expedition. They wondered if they could have saved lives after the avalanche by speeding to the bottom rather than combing the path.

They wondered how so many smart, experienced people could make the types of decisions that turned complex, rich, enviable lives into a growing stack of statistics.

Activity disturbed the quiet again. A Sno-Cat, a large machine with treads to climb through snow-covered terrain, rumbled through the trees below and parked at the bottom of the debris pile. Ski patrollers solemnly marched up the hill, carrying gear to wrap the bodies.

It was one deadly avalanche among many, perhaps no more worthy of attention than any other. It was not the nation's deadliest avalanche of the season. And it was not at all like the one that killed 96 people near Tunnel Creek more than a century ago.

But some rituals do not change. The accidents end with an unrefined ceremony.

Some patrollers stopped at Jack and wrapped him in a crude bundle using red blankets and rope. Others hiked to where Stifter and Carlsen sat. They wrapped the bodies of Brenan and Rudolph, with quiet expediency and reverence.

"I remember they said, 'There's no easy way to do this,'" Stifter said. "And they started slowly dragging them down the hill."

Donna's Dinner: In the Hard Fall of a Favorite Son, A Reminder of a City's Scars

New York Times

One in a Series of Five Articles

By Dan Barry

ELYRIA, Ohio

He walks the city streets with that block of a body angled headfirst, as if determined to break through life's defensive line. Often he is shouting with urgent intent, trying to tell the people of Elyria —something. But what?

He shouts about the father, the son and the Golden Helmet. About the time they killed his brother. About the baseball bat. About Les Miles, the Louisiana State University football coach, and a roster of other prominent Elyrians. His words tumble out like bits of broken thoughts.

But what is this man trying to say? As he weaves with purpose through City Hall, around Ely Square, in the front of Donna's Diner and out the back. As he talks so loudly that the owner, Donna Dove, has to tell him, Ike, Ike, use your inside voice or leave, which is like trying to lower the volume on a damaged radio.

Some people in Elyria try to help out; Ike Maxwell is one of their own. Judge James M. Burge and a lawyer, Michael J. Duff, give him money on a regular schedule, and a couple of Donna's patrons, from that front-table group called the Breakfast Club, occasionally hand him a few bucks. One day, he'll use the money to buy a meal; another day, a can of malt liquor.

But at 59, what is Ike trying to say? The truth is, some people know. Donna knows. So does Forrest Bullocks, a former city councilman who comes to her diner on Fridays for the perch special. Others know, too, that he is speaking in Elyrian about glory, regret and maybe even the one subject that vexes through boom and bust: race.

"Do you understand?" asks Ike, a black man, again and again.

DYNAMITE IKE

Unstoppable. Ike Maxwell on the high school football field was like an adult playing among children. A dominant, dazzling running back, he could stay on his feet no matter what hit him, and oh how he could run.

"Look at that. Look at that!" says Steve Sunagel, 57, a Breakfast Club regular and an old teammate of Ike's. "You can't teach that."

Steve, graying but still football fit, is watching a silent film of one game among many—Elyria vs. Lorain, Nov. 12, 1971—as the click of the reel ticks like a clock. There's No. 68, Les Miles. There's No. 47, Steve Sunagel. And there, forever finding daylight in the black-and-white past: No. 42, Ike Maxwell, running and scoring in a blowout against Elyria's archrival.

"See how he made that first guy miss," Steve says, excited. "He just gets through the tiniest of holes. A little shoulder shake and then. ... "

Ike electrified Elyria. During that 1971 season, the city ached for Friday night, when its very own celebrity was guaranteed to humiliate yet another rival. Home or away, thousands of Elyrians came to see every shimmy and shake of the phenom "Dynamite Ike."

Ike's father wasn't among them. He had been shot dead years earlier in a late-night gunfight at an Elyria bar. When the police found his body face down in the bar, he was holding a .22 revolver with three of its six cartridges spent. Ike was 12.

Nor was young, sandy-haired Donna Jacobson—Donna of the diner. A recent transfer from the overwhelmingly white Bay High School in Bay Village, she was a year behind Ike. She was so intimidated by the black students at Elyria High School that she cut nearly every class and eventually dropped out.

"I didn't know blacks," Donna recalls. "I was afraid of them."

But Ike's girlfriend, Beverly Wilson, was always there to shout his name. She had been Ike's biggest fan ever since junior high school, when they first met at a production of *Romeo and Juliet* at the Midway Mall.

"I'm ready to cry," Beverly says, her voice trembling over a telephone connection from a city far from Elyria. "He was so nice. He told me in ninth grade that he was going to break all the records."

Ike kept his word. He set school rushing records for most yards in a game, in a season, in a career. After he and Les Miles led the Pioneers to an undefeated 1971 season, Ike was All-Ohio and All-America and was given the award for the best football player and student in Lorain County. It's called the Golden Helmet.

"Everybody liked him," Beverly says. "He put Elyria on the map."

So many colleges came calling that *The Chronicle-Telegram* published a cartoon depicting recruiters beating on the young man's door. He eventually accepted a football scholarship to the University of Miami, where his future seemed like a clear field of green.

But the big time never happened for Ike; that is, it had already happened, in Elyria. After less than a year at Miami, he transferred to the University of Akron—to be closer to Beverly, he says—but did not stay long. Suddenly, he was just another former high school superstar, facing the hits and tackles of everyday life.

WHILE IKE STRUGGLED, ELYRIA ERUPTED.

Late one August night in 1975, two white police officers spotted a young black man climbing out a window of the Mayfair Tavern. As the suspect ran away, one of the officers ordered him to stop twice, and then fired his gun twice. A bullet to the back of the head ended the brief encounter.

The man was 19. He was carrying about 50 pennies, some cough drops and six packs of cigarettes. He was Daryl Maxwell, Ike's younger brother.

The Elyria police chief had explained that the department had a policy of "no warning shots," and that officers were trained to use their guns as a "last resort" to stop a fleeing suspect. If Daryl Maxwell had made it around the building, the chief said, "he would have been gone."

For two nights, hundreds of black people protested the shooting death by taking to the streets. Store windows were broken, firebombs thrown and shots fired in spasms of "racial violence," as *The Chronicle-Telegram* called it. Recalling those nights, Ike lowers his voice to say that he was so angry that all he wanted to do was throw rocks at the police—"like they did at Kent State."

By the second disturbed night, 41 people had been arrested, more than half of them white. Among those caught in the mayhem was Donna, 20 years old and living in a subsidized housing project. A thrown brick smashed her truck as she was trying to drive her two young daughters to safety.

During the rage-charged unrest, a black city councilman named Leo Bullocks—father of Forrest Bullocks—spent long hours driving around the city, talking to angry clutches of people, easing tensions. He could ease but never eliminate those tensions, especially when the authorities later ruled that the shooting death of the unarmed Daryl Maxwell was justifiable homicide.

Still, Leo did his part. Because he had standing, Forrest says, "they listened to him."

Leo Bullocks personified much of the Elyrian black experience. A Tennessee sharecropper with an eighth-grade education, he joined the great African-American migration north, seeking opportunity in the industrial boom that followed World War II. He chose Elyria because a relative had said jobs were sprouting there like bolls on a cotton plant.

Leo got a low-level job at the Harshaw Chemical Company, worked his way up to supervisor and made side money by driving a taxi and a dump truck. But he still found time to immerse himself in all things Elyria, from its Little League to its City Council, as if to gently but emphatically tell the white majority that this, now, was his home, too.

Leo was forever loyal to Elyria, Forrest says. "Elyria gave him a chance to reach his full potential."

When word spread in 1992 that Leo had developed lung cancer at the age of 70, after decades of chain-smoking Chesterfields, more than 250 people honored him at a country-club gathering at which the mayor wept for all of Elyria. And when he lay dying in a Cleveland hospital, Leo shared a few final words with his family, including this: "Tell Elyria that I love her."

Later that year, Leo's son Forrest was elected to the City Council. By now, Forrest had served four years in the Air Force during the Vietnam War, married and found a job in machinery repair at B. F. Goodrich that kept him busy enough. But he was also the son of Leo; he needed to serve his city.

DRUGS AND ERRATIC BEHAVIOR

By this time, another prominent resident of Elyria—one also deeply affected by the riot—had fallen hard: Dynamite Ike Maxwell.

Sometime around the time of his younger brother's death in 1975, Ike and his wife, Beverly, started an office-cleaning business. She remembers the fledgling company winning over some clients because they held her husband in awe. She said they'd ask: "Are you THE Ike Maxwell?"

But Ike struggled with drugs, alcohol and social navigation, she says, so much so that she left him, taking their children to another state. And things only got worse.

In the fall of 1980, a man repeatedly hit Ike in the head with a baseball bat at the Red Fox Lounge on Broad Street, causing multiple skull injuries. Five months later, he was shot and seriously wounded in the Showcase Lounge.

By the 1990s, Ike's name was appearing in the newspaper and in public records for reasons unrelated to his football exploits: criminal trespass, assault, harassment, possession of drug paraphernalia, possession of cocaine. Wandering the downtown streets, his shouts echoing off the ancient buildings, he now seemed to be playing on an entirely different field.

If Elyria has grappled with the Ike Maxwell of then and the Ike Maxwell of now, it has not been to Ike's favor. Though he was clearly one of the most dominant athletes the city had ever known, Ike has never been inducted into the Elyria Sports Hall of Fame—in part, a spokesman says, because its trustees also consider a candidate's moral character and contribution to the community.

At one point, Ike says, he even sold his Golden Helmet trophy to buy crack cocaine—then immediately felt bad about it. He says that with the help of a lawyer, Bill Balena, another regular at Donna's, he eventually retrieved the trophy and donated it to Elyria High School.

Over the years, a few of his former teammates have tried to help Ike, but he has worn out their patience with his erratic behavior. Sometimes, with the gentle counsel of, say, the lawyer Michael J. Duff, he can be calmed down long enough to talk thoughtfully about his life in Elyria. But too often he seems unable to follow a logical thread in conversation, or even to speak in a soft, level voice.

And when Ike shouts out the names of old teammates—Sunagel! Chlepciak! Miles!—you can't quite tell whether he does so in solidarity, or anger.

One of those teammates, Steve Sunagel, continues to watch the video of the Elyria-Lorain game of 1971 right to the end, when the undefeated team carries its coach, Bill Barton, off the field. But his pleasure in reliving football glory is tempered by his inability to reconcile the Ike he remembers and the Ike he sees today.

"Everything that all of us were—he was, too," he says.

STRAINS OF RACISM

Forrest Bullocks was elected to nine consecutive terms on the City Council, eventually serving as its president. He stepped down last year, but he serves as the Council's clerk and is involved with a civic booster organization called Main Street Elyria. He also visits every day with his mother, Mary, 89, who still lives in the modest house built by her Leo, after whom the city has named a ball field and a major roadway.

Sitting beside his mother in the family home, surrounded by photographs of the Bullocks family's journey from rural Tennessee to suburban Ohio, Forrest says race relations in Elyria remain a work in progress—nearly 40 years after the riot, and 60 years after Leo Bullocks first arrived.

Yes, it's true that the days when Forrest and his wife would be asked to leave a Las Vegas night at a private social club—even though it had been advertised in the newspaper as open to the public—are gone (though, he adds, "we haven't been back there since").

The racism is more nuanced now, he says, the mutual distrust more subtle and most often expressed behind one's back. Some white people still grumble when a black person is promoted. Some black people still dislike the police, seeing city life through the prism of the death of Daryl Maxwell, shot in the back of the head, pockets filled with pennies.

This is the country's constantly interrupted conversation, Forrest is suggesting, a conversation sometimes marked by tension, other times by hope, still other times by a silence mistaken for tolerance.

"We camouflage it better," Forrest says. "But there's still a lot of prejudice in Elyria. It is still here."

He says, for example, that African-Americans "know where we're welcome and where we're not"—though he adds that he and his wife, Gloria, will go to any restaurant in the city. One restaurant they prefer is Donna's, whose owner was once so determined not to be near black people that she dropped out of high school.

Donna is 57 now, and her attitudes about race have evolved, are still evolving, in fact. Her defenses began to break down when she was a scared young woman living in an Elyria housing project and an older black woman named Queenie took Donna under her wing. After that came all the time she spent with black co-workers and black customers—people she never would have encountered in Bay Village.

It's not as though Donna has experienced a we-are-the-world epiphany. "I took it slowly," she says, before adding, "I guess I grew up."

Now, on Friday afternoons, Donna can expect Forrest and Gloria Bullocks to arrive for their lake perch dinner. She will greet the couple with a hug, and when the food is served, she will sit and talk with them about anything and everything.

"The conversations go on like we've known each other for years," Forrest says.

Donna can also expect Ike to appear at any moment. He came into the diner not long ago, shouting again about the father, the son and the Golden Helmet, until she told him to quiet down. He said he had money—he receives disability and lives on a tight budget—and wanted to eat.

Ike ordered his usual meal: chef salad, steak, hash browns, rye toast and root beer. As usual, he used impeccable manners, his back erect. He ate in silence and, when he was done, left his usual good tip.

Then, with body at an angle, Dynamite Ike Maxwell left the diner to continue the never-ending conversation with his city, wandering its streets —and noticing, he says, how the whites still live here and the blacks still live there.

THE NATION'S POET

ATLANTA JOURNAL-
CONSTITUTION

By Rosalind Bentley

The National Book Festival along the Mall in Washington is thronged with readers and authors who've come to revel in the written word on this fall day in 2004.

Just three years old, the festival has been forged by first lady Laura Bush and the Library of Congress in the belief that literature is a living thing, that the right words, composed in just the right way, can push a life forward.

To the podium steps poet Natasha Trethewey.

Her work illuminates people in the shadows: a seamstress stitching her way through segregation; an early 20th-century prostitute so fair skinned she can pass for white; a dock worker's wife who keeps her husband's supper warm as she waits for him well into the night.

Into some of her poems she has woven her own complex story: the blending of the black and white blood that made her; her blood tie to her native Mississippi; the blood of her mother, cruelly spilled.

What binds the characters? It is that in the body of American letters, they have routinely been pushed to the edge of the page by other protagonists deemed more "universal." This day Natasha reads poems that bring their marginalized stories to the center.

"We peered from the windows, shades drawn,

at the cross trussed like a Christmas tree,

the charred grass still green. Then

we darkened our rooms, lit the hurricane lamps."

In the audience is Librarian of Congress James H. Billington. He is intrigued. Here is a beautiful woman, reading an elegant poem about the Ku Klux Klan burning a cross in her family's yard. Her poems are accessible, classic in structure, at turns gentle then brutal. Not often does Billington seek out a poet's work after a reading. With Natasha, he does.

2012: It's May. Natasha is the incoming chair of the creative writing program at Emory University and the newly minted poet laureate of her home state of Mississippi. She gets an unexpected call from the Library of Congress. Billington and his colleagues have been following her work since her first reading at the book festival. They are impressed with her 2007 collection, *Native Guard*. They are also taken with *Beyond Katrina*, her 2010 meditation on the psychological and structural wreckage dotting Mississippi's Gulf Coast landscape years after Hurricane Katrina's landfall.

Billington believes the time for this kind of poet is right now. She is only 46 and in the prime of her artistic life. This will signal that the library is looking forward. He offers her the highest United States honor a poet can achieve, poet laureate of the nation.

Saying yes isn't hard, though the honor humbles her, even makes her a little nervous.

The laureateship, officially the poet laureate consultant in poetry, is a congressionally mandated position of one to two years. Once a figurehead, anyone in the position now is encouraged to develop a program that interjects poetry into our daily lives.

Make the nation care about poetry?

What has this 46-year-old gotten into?

The shorthand of Natasha's life reads like words plucked from a free verse poem: Native Mississippian. Black mother. White father. Poet father. Poet daughter. Atlanta and DeKalb public school student. "A" student. UGA head cheerleader. Trauma survivor. Big sister. Decatur resident. Meticulous housekeeper. Proud wife. Exacting professor. Historical poet. Nobody's pushover.

She has publicly sketched the arc of her life in her poems, yet she is intensely protective of its sweetest moments. People can parse her work, even parse her appearance, but she will not tolerate parsing of the inner world she retreats to each evening with her husband.

"This is not a reality TV show," she says.

Fellow poets warn her about giving in to the relentless demands of the media as she moves forward. If she does, it will cripple her ability to create the art that got her here. They have also cautioned her about the pains, intended or not, that will be inflicted by critics. It galls Natasha that the press calls her a poet of race or memory.

"Memory. Race. Murder. That's what they say about me," she says. "I am an elegiac poet. I have some historical questions and I'm grappling with ways to make sense of history; why it still haunts us in our most intimate relationships with each other, but also in our political decisions."

In January she moves to Washington to serve her term at the Library of Congress. Even she says she is not certain how she will convince us to incorporate poetry into our daily routine.

For clues to how she may, we might look at how poetry came to matter in hers.

As Billington sees it, in a profoundly humane way, she has made heroes and heroines of forgotten Americans. They are often black, usually working class, indelibly Southern. In her words he also sees moments that remind him of the Brontë sisters. He appreciates her compulsion to wrestle with difficult questions of history that have roots in race, law and region. And he's compelled by the frankness with which she has dealt with grief that could have rendered her mute; all of this in five volumes that together are barely 2 inches thick. To Billington the stories Natasha tells are not simply hers but America's.

2. "IN 1965 MY PARENTS BROKE TWO LAWS OF MISSISSIPPI."

1966: Atlantan James Dickey becomes U.S. poet laureate in 1966, the year Natasha is born. Though his best known work will be the harrowing novel *Deliverance*, Dickey is first a poet. He writes of war, but also the South with its swaths of kudzu, where cars have panels that separate a "Lady and colored driver."

It is into this "colored" South that Natasha's life begins. Her mother, Gwen, is a coed at Kentucky State College, her father, Eric, a student athlete there and budding poet. Gwen is black, from Gulfport, Mississippi. Eric is white, from rural Nova Scotia, Canada. He has chosen the school because he is poor, the tuition is low and he can get an athletic scholarship. Plus, from the school brochure, the college looks integrated. That is until he sets foot on campus and realizes the students that appeared white in pictures were actually fair-skinned blacks. He has chosen a historically black college. Yet he stays.

Gwen is brown-skinned and lovely. He is taken with her performance in a school production of *Antigone*. She is struck that he has the courage to pledge a black fraternity. They date, binding themselves in poetry and each other. Their union is a symbol of the change in store for the nation. But at the moment they are still in the "colored" South. They are harshly reminded of it when Gwen becomes pregnant. There are statutes against interracial marriage on the books in Kentucky and when they try to marry, no one will help them break the law.

With their baby on the way they take a bus to Ohio to become Mr. and Mrs. Trethewey.

Their daughter will be 1 year old before the Supreme Court strikes down the nation's remaining anti-miscegenation laws.

Natasha is born in Gulfport on April 26, 1966, on the 100th anniversary of Confederate Memorial Day. Her early years are spent with her parents and her dark-skinned family in the segregated part of Gulfport.

Her extended Mississippi family is one of industry. Natasha's grandmother, Leretta Turnbough, is a seamstress. Her Uncle "Son" owns the local working man's bar. Natasha attends Head Start where her mother is an administrator. And Natasha's father works on the shipyard docks. In this house Natasha is doted on, absorbing the stories the adults tell to pass the time.

It's a joy she'll render years later in the poem "Collection Day."

"Saturday morning, Motown

forty-fives and thick seventy-eights

on the phonograph, window fans

turning light into our rooms,

we clean house to a spiral groove"

How nice it would be for Natasha if the world rocks on in such easy domestic rhythms. But the world demands choices. Black mother. White father. Black community. Who, then, does that make the child?

Some say, black child. The customs of Mississippi forbid, white child. The truth of her blood says, biracial child.

There is no acknowledgement in the culture, at least not now, that the racial middle ground is solid ground. America demands: Choose.

With light skin, hazel eyes and straight hair, a young Natasha tries to figure it out.

Sitting along the edges of conversation when her grandmother's friends are visiting, she is black child. Openly pitied by whites when she is with both her parents, she is biracial child. And sometimes, when she's on her own, the world sees her as white child. Sometimes she offers no correction.

The attempts at passing for white inflame her mother.

Anytime Natasha is caught telling a lie, Gwen makes her lick a bar of Ivory soap. As Natasha will later write in the poem, "White Lies," it is to "cleanse your lying tongue."

Life along the Gulf Coast provides Eric with plenty of inspiration for his own poetry. Tired of life on the docks, he enrolls in the University of New Orleans to get his master's degree, and then Tulane University for his Ph.D. He commutes back and forth. If he's in the car with his daughter he tells her to write what she sees to cut down on boredom.

Those early entries by Natasha may become lost to time. But at some point, the loving father, adored by his daughter, pens a poem with the line, "I study my cross-breed child." In his mind he means no harm. The phrase strikes Natasha as wrong. She is a smart child and knows that "breed" is a word used to reference animals. A crossing of breeds? Where does she fit in a scenario like that? Rather than ask the question she buries it deep inside. There the reference bruises and festers for nearly 35 years.

By 1972 Natasha's parents divorce under the strain of physical and emotional distance. Eric continues his academic path in New Orleans. Natasha and her mother move to Atlanta so Gwen can pursue her master's degree at Atlanta University.

Atlanta will bring opportunity, but it will also bring fresh pain, fuel for poems Natasha has yet to write.

. "I WAS ASLEEP WHILE YOU WERE DYING."

1976: It is a bicentennial year of firsts.

Robert Hayden is named poet laureate, the first African American to hold the post. Hayden is relentless in his insistence that his work is not race poetry, but American poetry, weft in the nation's literary fabric. To him, attempts to label it anything but American poetry are tantamount to artistic dismissal.

There is another poetic first this year. Natasha is 10 and has a poem published in the *Georgia Images and Reflections of Poets and Authors: Collected Bicentennial Year of 1976.* "Describing Animals," is the sort of rhyming, eight-line confection that makes a parent proud.

On the outside, Natasha's world looks like a shining example of the city's new black middle class. Her mother has finished school and is moving up the administrative ladder in social services. Gwen has remarried, this time to a black man, a Vietnam veteran and appliance repairman. They have had a son, Joe. Natasha spends summers in Gulfport with her grandmother and time with her father in New Orleans, where he is a college professor. She's a budding gymnast. In her predominantly black public schools, she writes poems about Civil Rights heroes. It doesn't happen in a single moment, but she knows she wants to be like the black women who reared her.

Natasha and her little brother pose for a picture around that time. It's the kind of studio portrait that comes to yellow over the years in the folds of a wallet. They appear happy.

The truth is that Natasha's stepfather is beating her mother and psychologically abusing Natasha. Gwen goes to work some days with bruises on her face. While she's there, sometimes he makes Natasha pack a bag, get into the car, then tells her he will take her to a center for the mentally "retarded." He drives her around until she nearly chokes on her tears. Only then does he take her home. She is in his house but she is not his child. She is a white man's child. And she is too scared to tell her mother of her torment.

She takes solace in her journal. When she suspects her stepfather is reading it behind her back, some of her entries grow defiant and profane. They are directed squarely at him. At this point she cannot know the depths of his capacity.

After 10 years, Gwen divorces her second husband. Through it all, she has steadily moved up the professional ladder, rising to personnel director for the DeKalb County Health Department. Her ex-husband stalks her.

On Valentine's Day 1984, he allegedly kidnaps Gwen at gunpoint as she leaves for work, forces her back into her apartment, beats her and repeatedly sticks her with a syringe full of battery acid. Police are notified after she does not show up for work. He is arrested and charged with attempted murder, but convicted of criminal trespass and gets a year in jail. As soon as he is released, his threats resume. Gwen, now 40, is put under police protection and her phone is wiretapped to record his threats. But there is a lapse.

On June 5, 1985, as his son waits outside for the morning school bus, the man appears, takes the 11-year-old's key and enters the apartment with the child. Gwen runs to the parking lot. He catches her. He punches her. Then he shoots her in the head.

She dies on the pavement.

Their son, who is in the apartment, is not physically harmed.

Natasha is away at school. The first reference of her in *The Atlanta Constitution* reads: "His wife leaves a daughter from her first marriage, Natasha, 19, a sophomore cheerleader at the University of Georgia."

He pleads guilty to murder and receives two consecutive life sentences in prison.

Natasha's brother, Joe, goes to live with his grandmother in Gulfport in the same house that was, for Natasha, a relatively happy one.

Back at UGA, she folds her grief into words on paper, though poetry remains a puzzle. She creeps back into campus life, even becoming the first black captain of the Bulldogs' cheer squad. In 1989, she graduates with an English degree.

Like Hayden, she will insist that her story is no less vital as she masters her art form.

4. SHE WRITES WHAT IS GIVEN TO HER TO WRITE.

1990s: Natasha pursues a master's in poetry at Hollins University in Virginia where her father now teaches. Years ago, on her visits to New Orleans, she would spend evenings listening to him and his friends debate points of literature and politics well into the night. It made her think she'd like to live a life of the mind. Now at Hollins, Eric suggests his daughter write a poem in the manner of "My Papa's Waltz," by Theodore Roethke. She writes the poem "Flounder," about a childhood fishing trip with her great Aunt "Sugar." The catch of the day yields an early lesson in what it might mean for her to navigate the world as biracial. One side of the fish is white, the other black.

In her backpack Natasha carries poet Rita Dove's *Thomas and Beulah*. Read one way, the work is about Dove's grandparents, for whom the book is named. Read another, it is the story of the Great Migration, the waves of blacks who left the Deep South between 1910 and 1970 for greater opportunities in the Midwest, North and West.

For Natasha the book becomes a template.

All around Natasha a new aesthetic is building. The black children of integration—no longer "colored"—are growing up and committing their stories to film, screen and books. Spike Lee is ushering in a new wave of black cinema. Visual artist Kara Walker is rattling sensibilities with her paper-cut murals on themes of race and the plantation South. Poet Elizabeth Alexander has her first collection published, *The Venus Hottentot*. In it, she draws a jagged line from Nelson Mandela, John Coltrane, her own Jamaican-American family, to the "Venus Hottentot," a 19th-century South African woman who was carted around Europe as a sideshow attraction. (Years later Alexander will deliver the poem at President Barack Obama's inauguration).

For these young artists, theirs is an expression of inherited blackness, but also a subtle reflection of the impact integration has had on their generation. The question is: What is this iteration of blackness?

Leading the charge in poetry is a group of African-American Ivy League students called the Dark Room Collective. Sharan Strange (who will later teach at Spelman College) and Thomas Sayers Ellis are its founders. Ellis says being a minority within a minority within a minority—black, Ivy-league, poetry student—is too rough to endure in isolation. Kevin Young (who will go on to be a National Book Award finalist and Emory University professor) is invited to join. So is Natasha, who is enrolled at the University of Massachusetts, Amherst in the MFA program.

They are rigorous with their sonnets, exacting in free verse, every one of them determined to join the canon. Each person represents, in some loose way, a different aspect of blackness not rooted in dogma. It's like jazz. Ellis invites Natasha because she helps, as he says, widen blackness, and that "there is balance in the widening." As their reputation grows they are invited to read up and down the East Coast, the *New Yorker* magazine and others take note.

For Young it's sort of like being in a garage band on the verge of a breakthrough. To him, when Natasha reads it's obvious she'll be a soloist.

But one of her graduate professors thinks she is sounding a false note.

The white instructor (a famous poet she refuses to name) tells her to stop writing about her dead mother and her blackness and to write instead "about the situation in Northern Ireland."

Choose.

His words scorch and by the time Natasha winds up in the office of her thesis adviser, author John Edgar Wideman, she is near tears. What is wrong with writing about aspects of the black experience, and are they not, by nature, the American experience? As American as those moments that inspired Flannery O'Connor's work? And is the story of her mother not that of one black woman, but also that of any woman who has ever raised children, worked hard, or had dreams that were erased? Wideman listens, having faced doubters himself as an African-American writer. He tells her that she has to write the truth and that the truth is her own story.

The situation in Northern Ireland is not hers to tell; the one in Gulfport, that is her story.

As the millennium closes, *Domestic Work*, Natasha's first collection of poems describing the world Wideman encouraged her to document, wins the inaugural Cave Canem Poetry Prize. It will become the most prestigious prize specifically honoring an African-American poet. The judge who selects the winner is Rita Dove, who won the Pulitzer Prize for *Thomas and Beulah* in 1987 and became U.S. poet laureate in 1993. When the two meet for the first time, Dove hugs her tightly. Their work has rendered them kin.

5. "HOW THE PAST COMES BACK."

2000s: The board lights up. Fellowships. Another book, *Bellocq's Ophelia*. Grants. A professorship. All the while Natasha continues to research and write, fusing neglected bits of history with her own. Not six years after winning Cave Canem, she submits a new manuscript to her publisher.

Some of the poems are about her mother; the pain of her suffering, her child's ache over her loss. Others are about the Gulfport years and the Jim Crow laws that menaced her family. Another set of poems is even more ambitious. They are based on a real, black, Civil War Union Army regiment sent to guard white Confederate prisoners of war on Ship Island off Mississippi's coast. She has spent months poring through archival records, photographs and documents of the period. To write from the soldiers' point of view she has had to inhabit their thoughts to make them flesh in verse. She says the volume, *Native Guard*, is therefore a monument to the marginalized and the forgotten.

It wins the 2007 Pulitzer Prize for poetry.

2012: Late August and Natasha is delivering the keynote address at the Decatur Book Festival. She is reading from her new book, *Thrall*. It is based on the famous "casta" paintings, which depict parsing of races in colonial Mexico—Indian, African, Spanish and the children of their unions. Into this she has layered poems about her father.

The words glide out of her, falling raw and tender on the listening ear.

"and I hear, again, his words—I study

my crossbreed child—misnomer

and taxonomy, the language of zoology."

As the stanzas build, some in the audience gasp. At the end, she tries to break the tension by encouraging the audience to email her father: "Tell him it wasn't that bad."

Her first book was dedicated "For my father," an appreciation, perhaps, for his encouragement of her talent. *Thrall,* is dedicated "To my father." He has written about her in his work for years. Now she addresses him directly.

They've read together at events, argued with each other, loved each other. Father and daughter is a tricky relationship to get right. The injury of "cross-breed child" must be dealt with.

"Breed means species," she says. "In that equation what species is my mother?"

If the phrase pierced her back then, it pierces him now that she's airing it in public.

He says he never meant to suggest his child was an animal, only that he sees her as a blend of the best of him and her mother; Arabian and quarter horse, he says. But "she gets it all tied up with the relationship between mule and mulatto. It's all wrapped up with her personal biracial identity, and I don't know whether she's able to be impartial about it."

Weeks later, she replies: "Daddy, you still don't hear what you're saying. It's just stunning to me."

Still, apart from *Native Guard*, her father calls *Thrall,* her best work yet.

There is a city-wide celebration for Natasha at the Decatur town square gazebo the day after her national laureateship is publicly announced. Natasha's father is there along with her husband, Brett Gadsden, an African-American history professor. Her brother, Joe, is in town to celebrate, too. Caught in the moment her father seems to float as high as she does. He says it's bigger than the Pulitzer, it's one of a kind. As hot as it is in the June sun, he pulls her gently against his barrel chest. She lets him cradle her and smother her with a huge kiss.

A stone's throw away from where they are standing is the courthouse where her mother's killer was sentenced.

Natasha is crying now, the source of her tears known only to her.

Sept. 13, 2012: The audience in the auditorium of the Library of Congress in Washington leaps to its feet. Applause crashes against the stage where a black woman in a dark dress stands, her hands clasped to her heart. Today, she looks as though she might burst with joy. This is U.S. Poet Laureate Natasha Trethewey, about to officially open the library's literary season with a reading. She has come to tell an American story.

"I Boy"

Milwaukee Journal Sentinel

December 2, 2012

By Mark Johnson

Isabella, a pink-cheeked lightning bolt in a Dora the Explorer shirt, uttered her first sentence around age 2; it was nothing her parents had expected. The two little words foretold a struggle over a fact of her birth.

"I boy."

When those two words had a chance to sink in, the child's mother, Jennifer, remembers thinking: Well, that might explain the interest in Matchbox cars. Maybe, Isabella just wanted to be like the other kids at day care; most were boys. Or maybe the child was simply confused.

At least it was only a phase, the mother told herself. It would pass.

That summer, clothes became a problem. Isabella kicked and screamed when Mom adorned her in pretty pink dresses. The child spilled salsa all over them, something that never seemed to happen when Isabella wore shorts and T-shirts.

Jennifer arranged her daughter's long brown hair in ponytails and pigtails, inserted bows and barrettes. And the first chance she got, Isabella yanked out the bows and freed her hair. When mom grabbed the brush, Isabella pushed her arm away.

When they shopped for clothes, Jennifer would hold up a dress, a sporty girls' outfit, a bright red T-shirt. No, said Isabella. No. No. Then came the tears. Then the walk over to the boys' department.

Don't you want to be a pretty girl, the mother would ask.

The child would not say, I want to run like a boy, or throw like a boy, or climb trees like a boy.

Just: "I boy."

One day last fall, two years after that first sentence, Jennifer made a decision. She took Isabella to Cost Cutters.

We need a short haircut, the mother said. I mean razor short. Like a boy.

She began dressing the child in boy's clothes.

Isabella became Izzy.

Of course, the name and haircut were just the beginning.

Gender dictates how we see children in the most fundamental ways— everything from the toys, books and clothes moms and dads buy, to the proms, weddings and other milestones they imagine. While girls and boys attend school together, they are conditioned to separation in bathrooms, locker rooms, gym classes, sports teams, even sections of the cafeteria.

These social conventions operate on a pair of assumptions: that there is always certainty about who is a girl and who a boy; and that every girl and every boy will look and feel and act the part.

But suppose you found yourself, as Jennifer did, dealing with a child who does not fit the assigned role—what would you do?

Her dilemma, while rare, appears more common than you might suppose. A large study of Dutch twins published in 2006 found that between 0.9% and 1.7% wished they were of the opposite sex. A national advocacy group estimates that between one-quarter of 1% and 1% of the American population—780,000 to 3.1 million people—believe they have been assigned the wrong gender.

Still, experts say there is really no reliable figure. The census does not have a category for people who live on these margins and even if it did, many would just as soon avoid the label—and the stigma.

One problem is that the public tends to confuse gender and sexuality. Desiring to be a different gender is not related to homosexuality. It isn't about sexuality, but identity, says John Kryger, chief of pediatric urology at Children's Hospital of Wisconsin and the Medical College of Wisconsin.

"Gender is who you go to bed as," he says. "Sexuality is who you go to bed *with*."

Blurring of the two may explain the visceral reaction many have to *transgender*, a word first coined in the 1960s and now used to describe people who have crossed, or wish to cross, the gender border. This dividing line is not, as we often assume, between the legs.

"Gender lives in the brain," says Stephen Rosenthal, medical director of the Child and Adolescent Gender Center at University of California, San Francisco. "Gender is defined as your perception of who you are."

J. Michael Bostwick, a professor of psychiatry at the Mayo Clinic, agrees that gender identity is "brain-based," but adds that researchers have yet to learn much about the specifics. "I think we have very crude instruments for looking at something that's very complex."

Children form their perceptions of gender very early in life, long before sexuality appears on the radar. The awareness arrives in stages. Even before 6 months, some babies can identify males and females by their faces and voices and can correctly connect the male voice to the male face, according to a 2011 paper in the journal *Social Science and Medicine*. It takes a little longer before children can label their own genders.

"It is my experience that very, very small children, when they get language, they speak up. Usually it is in between the first and second year," says Diane Ehrensaft, a clinical psychologist who has studied the subject for more than 40 years.

Genes play a role in gender identity. So do hormones. So does the brain. Upbringing, environment and culture may also play a part, according to some experts.

How all of these factors fit together is a mystery science is only beginning to unravel.

***

Even the language of gender, the vocabulary that confronts Izzy now and awaits in adulthood, is continually evolving.

The surgery to alter a person's gender has gone from "sex change," to "gender reassignment," to the politically correct-sounding "gender confirming."

People deeply unhappy with their sex are described as having "gender identity disorder," according to *The Diagnostic and Statistical Manual of Mental Disorders*. Families dislike the label, and its classification as a mental disorder. Yet many accept the diagnosis in order to receive medical services.

Editors of the manual are considering a recommendation to remove "disorder" and rename the condition "gender dysphoria" for the fifth edition, due out in May.[1]

The search for ways to explain the gender dilemma has proved equally unsatisfying.

"There's one very popular narrative, that someone has been born in the wrong body," says Scott Whipple, a clinical social worker in Manhattan who has spent more than 15 years studying gender identity. "I think it's very different for different people."

Izzy has been given a narrative. Borrowing loosely from American Indian legend, Jennifer told her child this story:

Twin spirits, a boy and girl, were waiting for a body.

Only one was available. The boy said, You go first. You have the body.

I can't be without you, said the girl.

The boy pushed the girl into the body, but at the last moment she dragged him in with her. The child was born with a girl body and a boy heart. The parents could see the girl.

They did not know about the boy inside.

***

The first to know about Izzy were not Jennifer and her husband, Diego, who had, by then, separated.

Instead, the boy appeared to big sisters Yasmine (or Yazzy), who is nine years older, and Angeliah (or Angel), who is five years older. There were hints in Isabella's rough style of play, but it was really "the game" that clued in the sisters.

The older girls would ask Isabella, Are you a boy or a girl?

It was funny because whatever they said last—that's the one Isabella picked.

Not quite 2, the child seemed lovably confused. After a while, though, Isabella's answer never wavered.

Boy.

Mom, the girls called. Look!

They showed her how Isabella answered. It had to be deliberate; when they pointed to other children, Isabella knew who was a boy and who was a girl.

The older girls thought about how Isabella played when they took their dolls out in strollers. Yazzy and Angel were gentle with the dolls. Isabella? She rammed the stroller around their Monona house, fast as a race car.

Jennifer had noticed the way Isabella roared into the living room making explosion sounds and firing pretend lasers.

The toys, the play style, the game, they were all signs. The sentence was a declaration.

"I boy."

***

Boy and girl seem such easy concepts in high school biology. A single pair of chromosomes settles the question—XX and you're a girl; XY, you're a boy.

But it's not that simple. A complex cascade of genes and hormones during the first 12 weeks in the womb determines whether we develop the gonads, internal ducts and external genitals of a male or a female.

Sometimes biology sends mixed signals.

A child can be born with the Y chromosome, yet develop as a woman. In a condition known as androgen insensitivity syndrome, the child is born with a mutation that sabotages a gene. The gene is supposed to make receptors for male androgen hormones to bind onto. But the mutation disables the receptors. The androgens have no place to go.

Without androgens, the body is blind to the Y chromosome. Sexual features develop as if the child were a girl. At puberty, the child appears female, but has no uterus and no monthly period. If this were not confusing enough, the syndrome has a "partial" version, which can result in ambiguous genitals.

Mother Nature spins other variations.

Some children are born with a mutation that disrupts development of the hormone cortisol. The chemical that is supposed to become cortisol is instead diverted down the pathway that fires up production of male hormones. The body is flooded with testosterone and other male hormones. The condition occurs in both boys and girls, but only affects genital development in girls.

A girl with the mutation has ovaries. She also has "masculinized" genitals, which can range from an enlarged clitoris or partially fused labia to a penis and scrotum.

The result: a child who looks like a boy but isn't. Long-term studies have found that most of these children end up choosing to live as females, but roughly 1 in 20 chooses to be male.

Such mutations are rare. Most people with gender conflicts never know the cause.

Comminglings of male and female are unusual, but not unnatural. The animal kingdom includes types of zebra finches and butterflies that are essentially half and half. The butterflies have a male color pattern on one wing, a female pattern on the other. Biologists don't know what causes the rare phenomenon of half-male/half-females, known as gynandromorphs. They suspect genes play some role.

There is an important difference, though, between the male-female mixes in the human world and those in the rest of the animal kingdom. In most of nature, male and female are concepts largely confined to mating behavior.

"Humans are a unique case," says David Crews, a professor of zoology and psychology at the University of Texas at Austin. "The issues about transgender, gender identity and role preferences—those are all human concepts. In animals all you can say is that there are alternative reproductive strategies."

The human concepts support the idea that at some deep level gender identity resides in the brain, a point reinforced by a few recent studies.

A 2011 paper in the *Journal of Psychiatric Research* examined the white matter, or connecting fibers, in the brain. Scientists found that in transsexuals desiring to go from female to male this tissue was already more similar to that of a man before any treatment.

A 2009 study published in the journal *NeuroImage* examined gray nervous tissue in the brain, comparing male-to-female transsexuals with control males and control females. Although the transsexuals most closely resembled other males, the authors wrote that one section of the brain, the putamen, "was found to be feminized," in transsexuals.

***

For now, Izzy is a mystery.

There has been no test to determine whether there might be a biological explanation for the child's gender dilemma.

Jennifer's feeling is that the causes are not as important now as how Izzy behaves and is treated by others. If doctors find no telltale mutations or hormone problems, it will not change the child's insistence. Such things mean nothing to a 4-year-old. Nor do they change the child others see.

Izzy has broad shoulders, friendly brown eyes and a layer of childish pudge that for some reason looks "male." The child is shy with strangers, but playful. Izzy likes Spider-Man, cars, football, fire engines, tool benches and Star Wars LEGO video games.

Once, the mother caught her child trying to stand at the toilet. The clothing, the floor, the child's legs—everything was wet. Izzy, then 3, was upset.

Jennifer grabbed Diego, who was at the house, and had him explain that boys sit down on the toilet too.

She wondered: Does Izzy realize that standing won't work because the genitals are wrong? Or does Izzy think poor potty skills are to blame?

The truth is she cannot be certain how much her child understands.

One day recently the mother asked: "What do you want people to call you?"

"Izzy."

"What is your name?"

Long pause.

"Why did Mom name you Isabella?"

Silence.

"Is Isabella a girl name or a boy name?"

Finally an answer.

"Boy name."

On another day, there was no pause. Jennifer was rearranging the living room, moving the framed photographs of the children on the wall when Izzy pointed at one.

That's when I was a girl, the child said.

***

The before-and-after world that Izzy sees is more difficult for a mother to explain. Whenever Jennifer discusses her child's gender, she always faces one question.

How do you know?

The mother has a standard response: When you were 4, did you know you were a girl? Did you know your father was a boy? Well, that's how Izzy knows. The same way.

But how do you know?

After all, parents don't take a child's word when deciding whether it's safe to play with matches. Why follow the judgment of a 4-year-old?

Izzy has been diagnosed with gender identity disorder. A doctor has judged that for at least two years Izzy has been strong and persistent in rejecting the female gender.

No dresses. No dolls.

Fire engines and footballs.

How do you know? What if a 4-year-old is strong and persistent now, but later reverses course?

"I've seen a lot of children who mislabel themselves when they're young," says Ken Zucker, head of the Gender Identity Service at the Centre for Addiction and Mental Health in Toronto. "Lots of these children can be helped to feel better about the gender that matches their birth."

To get some idea of how young children understand development, ask them this: If you grow long ears, will you grow up to be a rabbit? Many will say "yes," Zucker explains.

Several studies have found that less than 20% of the children who experience severe unhappiness with their assigned gender continue to feel this way during and after puberty. However, a 2011 study in the journal *Clinical Child Psychology and Psychiatry* reached a dramatically different conclusion: about 55% of the children surveyed maintained discomfort, and many reported that the feelings intensified.

Izzy's mind might change, Jennifer says. But it will be Izzy's mind. Better to deal with a change down the road than to force a child into a despised role.

Jennifer did not wish for this. It bothers her to think how much harder her child's life could be.

It bothers her that the transgendered have a much higher suicide rate than the general population (about 40% of transgender people have attempted suicide, a recent survey found). It bothers her too that fulfilling a wish to be fully male may shorten Izzy's life span (testosterone treatments can raise cholesterol and blood sugar, and surgery comes with a high risk of complications, according to the American Psychological Association).

Moreover, as a male, Izzy would be sterile. Having children would be possible only by keeping the uterus and ovaries intact—by, in effect, taking advantage of the sex previously abandoned. The mother wonders if Izzy will be old enough at puberty to appreciate the significance of being unable to have children.

In her view, the questions and uncertainties boil down to a single test: What does a mother do to love her child?

***

In public, gender sheds its complexity. We don't see the genes, the brain, the upbringing, the things that live inside us. We see what's on the outside. We see clothes and a haircut.

For Isabella, the clothes came first. Jennifer dressed the child in boy clothes but left the hair long, sometimes in pigtails. The mother agonized.

She wept as she talked with her sister. The world would judge her decisions about Isabella.

The world be damned, her sister said. You know your child. Nothing you're doing cannot be undone.

The crucial change took place in October 2011 as Isabella's fourth birthday approached. The child asked for a haircut. Jennifer and Isabella looked in a book and found a photograph of a boy haircut. They showed it to the stylist at Cost Cutters.

Jennifer worried the stylist would try to talk them out of it, or even refuse service. The mother listened to the sound of the scissors and clenched her fingers. Jennifer looked down and saw her knuckles growing pale.

Then she looked at her child.

Shorter? she asked.

The child smiled. The stylist kept cutting.

"As his hair got shorter and shorter, his smile got bigger and bigger," Jennifer recalls. "I think that's when I finally got it."

***

Izzy celebrated a new self by dressing for Halloween as Darth Vader.

For others in the family, the change brought a mourning period. Diego said he thought about the traditional Latin American quinceañera celebrating a girl's 15th birthday. He thought of the beautiful dress he would never see descending from Isabella's shoulders.

Yazzy and Angel missed Princess Day. That's what Jennifer called the day when she would gather her daughters, buy earrings for all three, take them to a hair salon, then have their photograph taken.

"That pretty much ended," Angel said.

Subtle adjustments ran deep.

The two older girls stumbled over pronouns, calling Izzy "she," catching themselves, switching to "he." The mother faced a similar problem. "I had to change," said Jennifer. "I said, 'my girls.' Now it's 'my kids.' "

He or she?

The pronouns loomed on the horizon, on the school paperwork Jennifer would have to file when Izzy entered kindergarten for 4-year-olds; it was less than a year away. Pronouns would be important in class. Teachers had to know how to refer to Izzy. Pronouns would determine which line the child stood in for the bathroom.

In 2012, Jennifer picked a pronoun. She began to fill out "male" on all of the forms for school, youth soccer, anywhere someone wanted to know Izzy's sex.

She decided to send Izzy to the Madison schools instead of those in Monona. Madison, she felt, was better prepared to deal with her child. During the summer a representative from a California nonprofit, Gender Spectrum, had flown out to Madison to train school staff for two days on gender issues. The staff discussed everything from handling gender on school forms to creating classrooms that are comfortable for all the children, including those who find themselves outside the gender norms.

"The district has just been incredibly thoughtful about this," the group's director of education and training, Joel Baum, said after his visit. "It was not even a matter of: Are we going to do this? It was: How are we going to do this?"

Even so, Jennifer said she worried: What am I forgetting? How will my choices to do this or not do it affect Izzy?

One of those choices was the decision to tell Izzy's story. She wanted there to be a story out there for other moms that would tell them, "Here's what you have to prepare for, but don't worry. It can be OK."

At the same time, she thought about Izzy at 15, at 18, at 21, and imagined a potential employer running a computer search of Izzy's name, finding this article and discriminating against her child. She realized that in trying to help other families with transgender children she might harm her own. The idea upset her terribly. She changed her mind. She insisted that the *Journal Sentinel* not include the family's last name.

The decision brought home just how exhausting and scary Izzy's journey has been, a point Jennifer was determined to see that school officials understood. So she went to a meeting of Madison Metropolitan School District principals. She brought a PowerPoint presentation.

The first slide showed a recent photo of her smiling, short-haired child. The photo was labeled "My Son."

Other photos showed a progression: a baby "born a girl"; a little girl who seemed unhappy in a dress; a child who wore Spider-Man outfits and baseball caps; a kid who played with hammers, drills, wrenches. The child in the photos looked less and less like a little girl.

"Now try thinking if this was your child . . ." one of the slides said. "Think about constantly defending your choices and their right to exist . . . I love my son no matter what. I think if you were me you would too. Please, I need compassion and support. My son is entering 4K this year and I am scared to death . . . "

***

A month of school passed, then a second. So did some of the fear.

There is a unisex bathroom that the child uses. The mother has been low key, telling only the school's principal about Izzy.

So far, none of the teachers have said anything about gender. Jennifer suspects they know about Izzy. Like many 4-year-olds, Izzy still has the occasional accident.

But none of the other children have asked Izzy awkward questions or made hurtful comments. The child has been free to make friends, sing songs, learn letters and numbers and take part in all of the other routines of kindergarten.

"People have been waiting years and years for policies to protect their kids," Jennifer said, "and we get to walk into it."

After school one afternoon, Izzy went to soccer practice for 3- and 4-year-olds. There were eight girls, six boys and Izzy.

The children scampered across the field, stumbling into each other's paths, chasing the coaches, sometimes winding up inside the goals. Jennifer watched Izzy, a lightning bolt in a soccer shirt.

As her eyes followed the child, the image registered in her mind:

"A boy," she said.

1. DSM-5 was published in May 2013. It does indeed replace "gender identity disorder" with "gender dysphoria" to describe "the distress that may accompany the incongruence between one's experienced or expressed gender and one's assigned gender." It is meant to focus "on dysphoria as the clinical problem, not identity per se."— Editors

Young Houstonians Go from Homelessness to College

The Houston Chronicle

July 22, 2012

By Monica Rhor

That first night, surrounded by strangers, still shell-shocked after her family was cast onto the street, Tiara Reado shrank back into childhood. The teenager stayed glued to her mother's side, following her around the Star of Hope shelter like a toddler.

When the older woman stirred, Tiara stirred with her, whispering, "Mommy, where are you going? Mommy, I'm coming with you."

Then Tiara cried. She cried when they had to camp on the floor, next to dozens of other homeless families. She cried when they moved into a cramped room with narrow cots and cinderblock walls. She cried when she realized they had no place else to go.

For seven days straight, she cried.

What else can you do when you're 16 and your dad is out of work and your family has just been evicted? What else can you do when you're just a kid—scared and sleepy and hungry?

A few months later, Courtney Williams was huddled on the floor of the same shelter, sharing space with the unknown and clutching his Bible.

The 17-year-old's family had just been kicked out of their apartment. His mother had been very sick for a very long time and he was on the verge of dropping out of school. The whole world, it seemed, was conspiring against him.

So, Courtney bowed his head over the Book of Proverbs, sobbed quietly and prayed. All night long, he cried.

What else could he do?

On those dark nights of tears, when everyday teenage dreams were displaced by uncertainty, Tiara and Courtney cried for the homes they lost, the proms they wouldn't attend, the colleges they couldn't afford. What they didn't yet know was that, sometimes, falling into shadow will lead you to the light.

***

With its boxy industrial-green exterior and pungent ammonia-cleaner smell, the Star of Hope Women and Family Emergency Shelter is a place of last resort, a safety net for those in a downward spiral—and a hard gulp for families losing the fight for subsistence.

"When people come here, they are acknowledging that they can't make it on their own," said Marilyn Fountain, Star of Hope's director of community relations. "There's a certain kind of humiliation that comes with that. It's a tough place to be."

Tough enough for the adults who trudge through the doors, clasping plastic bags stuffed with belongings and carrying the slight shrug of defeat on their shoulders.

Much tougher still for the children. Some too young to understand. Others, like Tiara and Courtney, old enough to feel the keen edge of fear and embarrassment.

On any given day, more than half of the 300 people crowded into the emergency shelter are under age 18. Of the 600 people staying in various Star of Hope facilities, about 200 are children.

"They have no control over their circumstances. They didn't create it and they can't change it," said Fountain. "Children live more in the moment, and the moment in which they are living is fraught with images of deprivation."

That moment doesn't last forever. But when you're a teenager, and life has been full of bumps and bruises and blows, it can feel like an eternity.

***

By the time Tiara and her family landed at Star of Hope in the summer of 2010, the good years of her early childhood had dissolved into a long patch of bad.

In middle school, taunts about boys from mean girls escalated into a cycle of fights and suspensions, turning school into a gauntlet of bullying. When she was about 13, Tiara was sexually assaulted by a boy she liked, a trauma she kept hidden for months.

Then, her father, a sandblaster who works out of state, was hurt on the job and had no way to support the family. Bills piled up. Rent was overdue.

One day, Tiara's mother sat her down and told her they had been evicted.

"Ma, where are we going? Is there a house I don't know about?" Tiara asked, feeling lost, confused, and achingly useless.

At first they stayed with Tiara's grandmother, but after a disagreement, they were on the streets again.

Tiara searched on Google for family shelters and stumbled onto Star of Hope.

At her first glimpse of the Women and Family Emergency Shelter, Tiara burst into tears. Strangers were everywhere: weary mothers pushing strollers, unkempt women muttering to themselves, wary and skittish teens like herself.

Tiara didn't want to be there. And she didn't want her classmates at Phillis Wheatley High School finding out her address was now an emergency shelter.

Kids will talk about you until it hurts, Tiara had learned long before. Even if you're not homeless, even if you have a place to stay. They will talk and it will hurt.

So, she didn't tell anyone except the school principal and her closest friends. She was the first one picked up on the bus route in the morning, and the last one dropped off in the afternoon. She raced to keep the laundry room time slot assigned to her family, just to have clean clothes to wear.

Through it all, Tiara kept her sorrows masked.

She laughed loudly and acted crazy and smiled her big, incandescent smile. But behind that vivacious facade, the worries circled like sharks: When are we going to get out of this? When is it going to get better?

***

That's what Courtney was asking himself as well.

In the fall of 2010, while Tiara was trying to hide her homelessness, Courtney was scraping and scrambling to keep his family afloat.

The previous year, around winter break, the then-high school freshman had come home to find his mother, younger brother and sister gone.

All Courtney found was a note on the door, telling him to get the key from a neighbor.

For several days, he sat alone. He watched Christmas come and go by himself. Then he found out that his mother, who was raising the family on her own, had been rushed to the hospital and was gravely ill.

Suddenly, Courtney was thrust into the roles of cook, housekeeper and breadwinner. He mowed lawns, fixed bikes, did whatever it took to raise a few dollars. He looked after his siblings, and when his mother was released from the hospital unable to walk, Courtney took care of her, too.

And the boy who had kept up his grades during a childhood spent bouncing from one apartment to another, who loved math and science and poetry, who longed to be an aerospace engineer, desperately tried to keep from falling behind in school.

But it was like a steep climb up a crumbling mountain.

Courtney missed days of school to nurse his mother. He turned in projects late because there was no money for simple supplies like poster board or markers. He failed classes but couldn't afford the bus fare to get to credit recovery courses.

His teachers at Yates High School didn't believe his excuses and accused him of slacking off. One day Courtney pushed his mother to school in a wheelchair to prove he was not inventing her illness.

Courtney's mother watched her baby flail, and she felt her heart shred. Courtney watched his grades slip, and he felt ground down.

"I'm not a bad person," he would think to himself. "So why do bad things keep happening?"

Still, Courtney held onto the one thing that had never deserted him: his faith.

The kid who once was teased for being a "church freak" because he went to services and Bible study four or five times a week grasped tightly to the Good Book. Over and over, he read Proverbs 3:5–6: "Trust in the Lord with all your heart and lean not on your own understanding."

And he went to Hope for Youth, a ministry for teens grappling with poverty, homelessness and hard times.

It was there one day, while playing a game of Connect Four, that he met a lanky, bright-eyed girl whose flashing smile was shaded by tears.

Tiara.

***

They became instant friends. This girl with her troubles tucked behind a bubbly exterior; this boy with his troubles etched plainly on a solemn demeanor.

The kind of friends who exchange texts late at night, call just to make sure everything's OK, write each other's names in notebooks. The kind who understand when no one else does.

For Tiara, Courtney became a lifeline in the storm, the voice in her head telling her not to give up, never to give up.

When her classmates found out she was homeless. When her baby sister's first birthday was celebrated in a shelter. When teachers didn't believe what she was going through.

When dancing and music and journal-writing weren't enough to wipe the worries from her mind.

Courtney was there, even as his world was in tatters.

I'm going through this with you; you're not alone, he would assure her. God puts us through things so we can grow in faith, he would counsel. In time we'll understand and eventually things will get easier, he would soothe, sounding far wiser than his years.

So, Tiara brushed off the bullies and the bad days. Her thoughts of dropping out dissipated. And she plunged herself into homework and extra credit, determined to catch up in school and to prove those who doubted her wrong.

This is just one part of my life, she wanted to tell the teasers and taunters. I haven't even begun to start living.

***

In the early months of 2011, Tiara's father had found work again, her family had moved out of the shelter, and she was on track to graduate.

But just as Tiara's roadblocks began to clear, the ground opened up beneath Courtney's feet.

Courtney, then in his junior year, discovered he had slipped so far behind in school that he was classified as a freshman. All his hard work, all the hours spent studying, had been for nothing.

One afternoon, Courtney and his siblings came home from church camp to find their belongings packed in boxes. His mother, sitting hunched at a table, was in tears. The family had been evicted and had nowhere to go.

A smile stayed fixed on his face, but inside Courtney felt his faith ebbing away.

He raced to give the family's furniture away to people who had even less. He lobbied for a place in the Star of Hope's emergency shelter, competing with dozens of other families in the same straits.

That night, in the summer of 2011, Courtney found himself sleeping on the tile floor of the shelter. He opened his Bible to a verse about a man who cried out to God, and in the morning, has his cries answered.

And so it was.

The next morning, Courtney and his family got a room in the shelter. It was, he realized, the first step in inching out of the darkness.

One of the first things Courtney did was to reach out to other teenagers at the shelter, who were too embarrassed to go outside, too ashamed to let anyone see that they were homeless. He let them know they were not alone.

Over the next year, Courtney managed to catch up on his classes by staying after school for hours, churning out homework assignments, and begging for extra credit. He signed up for Advanced Placement courses. He got to know the students on the University of Houston debate team, who volunteer in the shelter cafeteria, and tagged along to tournaments.

There, he caught the eye of UH officials, who were so impressed that they offered Courtney a full scholarship.

For a split second, when he first heard the news, Courtney was afraid it was an illusion that would evaporate upon waking. Soon, however, the disbelief transformed into a grin that wouldn't quit.

On June 2, Courtney marched across the stage to receive his diploma from Yates High School. He cried. His mother, sitting in the audience, screamed with delight.

Two days later, Tiara got a diploma of her own from Furr High School's REACH Charter, where she transferred after leaving Star of Hope.

The best friends, who once shed tears on the same shelter floor, now see Star of Hope as a lucky misfortune.

It is a place that caught them as they were falling, and led them to each other.

"She's like me. I can tell her everything," says Courtney, 18, whose family still lives in the shelter's Transitional Living Center. "Even though we were both going through hard times, we leaned on each other and gave each other comfort and advice."

Times are still tough, and their families still scuffle to stay on solid footing, but these days, the light edges out the darkness.

In the fall, Courtney plans to enter UH, pursuing his goal of becoming an aerospace engineer. Tiara is taking classes at Houston Community College and hopes eventually to open her own dance studio.

Both want other people to know that the face of homelessness is not always what you think.

"People think when you're homeless, you have nowhere to go, you have no food, you're in dirty clothes all the time, and you're living under a bridge," says Tiara, 18. "But homeless is not just someone standing on the street with a sign."

Sometimes, homeless is a young girl with sparkling eyes and a contagious laugh or a young boy who loves math and science and poetry. And, sometimes, homeless doesn't have to last forever.

THE GIRL WHO TOOK DOWN THE GANG

THE VIRGINIAN-PILOT

DECEMBER 23, 2012

By Louis Hansen

A young man was beaten to death by gang members who had been terrorizing Norfolk. Skyler Hayward's testimony proved vital to putting many of them in jail. During five years in solitary confinement, she gained perspective – and a mentor and friend.

NORFOLK

The lawyer backed his Mercedes SUV into a reserved spot close to the exit of Norfolk City Jail.

Sheriff's deputies he'd known for decades asked him for identification.

Tucked between a clutch of officers, a young woman emerged from behind a brick wall. She wore a new blue sweatsuit.

"I told you I'd get you out," the lawyer, John Coggeshall, said.

Skyler Hayward smiled, filled her lungs with fresh air and climbed into the passenger's seat.

Coggeshall swung the Benz into traffic and toward the highway.

They fell into an easy silence.

Coggeshall had handled dozens of murder cases, but he had never driven a getaway car. He stared into the rear and side mirrors. Were they being followed?

The wind poured through the open windows and sunroof on a pristine June day this year. Hayward twisted up the volume for Beyonce. She painted her toenails.

She wanted something good for her first meal, she told him.

That's what you'll get, Coggeshall said. He added to himself: If we get out of here alive.

Coggeshall had just turned 57. After a career as a touring nightclub singer, he had spent nearly two decades as a criminal defense lawyer. He fought hard for his clients, but most were guilty, and few seemed redeemable. Nearing retirement, he craved little more adventure than a Virgin Islands rum cigar and an Irish coffee.

He glanced over at his charge: Her round, girlish face and inquisitive eyes. Court records described her this way: Member of the Bounty Hunter Bloods, convicted of first-degree murder, robbery and malicious wounding.

Coggeshall saw something different: "The most courageous woman I've ever known."

Five years earlier, Hayward had stared for the first time at the steel door of a solitary confinement cell on the third floor of the Norfolk jail. She had pleaded guilty to murder. No deal with prosecutors.

The case was brutal and notorious. Three friends were lured to a deserted parking lot, robbed and beaten. Two of them, Navy sailors, escaped. James Robertson, 19, lay motionless, dying. The robbery netted $12.

Within 48 hours, Skyler Hayward broke with the gang.

She knew the risk.

Bounty Hunter Bloods ran Ocean View, Norview and more. Gang snitches and enemies were shot, burned with irons or tortured if they were lucky enough to escape execution.

In the weeks following the fatal beating, Hayward's brother was abducted, and a fire was set at her mother's home.

She also knew she could not hide, even in jail.

Anonymous letters arrived laced with threats.

When she walked down the corridors in chains, she heard the talk: "Gonna cut your throat." "Dead man walking."

Hayward stared at the door of that cell. She had no idea when, or if, it would ever open.

She was 17.

Skyler Hayward grew up in the Midwest, living mostly with her grandparents, she said. Her mother worked a series of jobs, including hairdresser, but also piled up a criminal record. Her father has spent much of his adult life in prison.

She moved to Virginia for high school to join her brother, Gerard Jr., and her mom. The switch from the country made Norfolk seem like Vegas.

Granby High School was like college to her.

At first, Hayward went to classes regularly, even when she found them boring. A few teachers inspired and encouraged her. She liked to read, but not always the books assigned at school.

As a teen in a new city, she was lonely, sometimes awkward. Her mother juggled jobs at two supermarkets, leaving Hayward and her brother free time. When she was upset, she'd slip out of her mom's home near Ocean View, cut through a few streets to the beach. At night, on the sand, just the waves crashing, she dreamed of cruise ships and traveling the world.

She struggled to make friends, but she got along well with boys. She was a tomboy in some ways.

Her brother introduced her to his friends. Gerard, a year older than Skyler, was already a gang member, she said.

Soon, her favorite part of high school was the bus stop in front.

Hayward skipped classes after a few periods, rode the HRT bus a couple of miles to a shopping center and hung out with friends, some gang members. They smoked—somebody always had weed—and chilled until it was time to go home.

She learned the gang rituals, the coded language and the life. A male friend pressured her to join. "Get with it, or get beat up," other members told her.

Hayward resisted, but not for long.

One night, she waited on the stoop of her house with some friends. In a dark lot across the street, a group of female gang members, known as rubies, planned the ritual.

Five girls peeled off into a circle. Hayward was brought over and thrown in. The young women punched, kicked and shoved her. At 31 seconds, it was over.

Skyler Hayward, 16, member, Bounty Hunter Bloods. She called herself "Lil' Drama" because she didn't make a scene.

Once in the gang, Hayward discovered she was expected to be around, even at the expense of the part-time jobs she held. They wanted her recruiting new girls and paying monthly dues of $10 or $20.

One night, her friend Shakida Bowers called, she said, and was strapped for money. Bowers was pregnant.

James Robertson, a cousin and friend of two sailors stationed in Norfolk, called the girls. They had met him a few weeks earlier and exchanged numbers. The men wanted to get together.

They met in a parking lot at 16th Bay Street in Ocean View. It was a hot Friday night, July 27, 2007.

Police arrested Hayward at a Norfolk hotel with other gang members. She was the first to tell them what happened. She admitted later in court that she didn't tell the entire truth the first time, but a consistent account emerged. Details from her statements and court testimony piece together a set-up, robbery and attack:

The men drove to the parking lot expecting to meet the girls for a party.

A gang member sat in the back of a pickup truck while several girls greeted Robertson and his friends.

When all three men had gotten out of their vehicle, Curtis Newby, from the back of the pickup, waited and watched. A group of men swarmed from behind an apartment house.

Newby pulled a gun, Hayward told police. "He tells them to get down on the ground just like cops tell people to get down on the ground."

A few girls, but not Hayward, she testified, rifled through the men's pockets and searched their truck.

"Me and one of the other females, Shakida, we yelled 'cops,' " Hayward said to police. "It was a false alarm, a little bit of people scattered a little bit, but they came back. That's when they started beating them with a gun."

"I was still in the midst of being drunk and everything. I still, everything, I saw everything, but it was just like slow, like it was like slow. I was dumbfounded. I see it, but it was slow."

"It just happened," Hayward said. "It just ended up happening."

Three days later, Coggeshall was working the duty shift at Norfolk Juvenile and Domestic Relations Court. Lawyers waited to be called over the loudspeaker to meet and represent poor clients.

A bailiff told Coggeshall to report to courtroom four. He arrived to find a baby-faced teen in a jail sweatsuit, her wrists and ankles shackled. Skyler Hayward looked scared.

"A curfew violation?" he thought.

The judge recited the most serious charge: first-degree murder. Coggeshall handed Hayward a card and explained that the court had appointed him to represent her.

She nodded and said nothing. "Don't worry," Coggeshall said, "we'll see this through."

Coggeshall had offered similar words to hundreds of clients. He hadn't gotten close to any of them.

Coggeshall knew nothing about the case. Police released few details publicly. But the lawyer quickly realized its importance. Then-Norfolk Commonwealth's Attorney Jack Doyle and other senior prosecutors and investigators buttonholed Coggeshall outside courtroom four.

Hayward had begun to cooperate, but they wanted more.

Before she talked to police, she said her mom gave her some advice: "Do what you have to do. Don't go down for anybody else's crime."

Hayward asked, "If I tell, will you be able to handle it?"

"We'll be OK," her mother said.

Shivering in an icy interrogation room, wearing a hooded T-shirt, skirt and flip-flops, Hayward waived her right to an attorney and delivered a sworn statement about the killing. She was not even the youngest of the suspects. They ranged in age from 15 to 29.

Hayward was different. Her older brother had taught her how the gang worked. She also dated a cousin of one of the generals, known as "Big Homies." She was street-smart without being hardened, her lawyer said.

Norfolk police and prosecutors had been pursuing the various sets of the Bounty Hunter Bloods.

A confidential 2008 state police intelligence report warned that the Bloods, or BHB, were "particularly violent," and their activities included "assault, kidnapping, drug dealing, illegal firearms possession, murder and robbery."

Gang members went so far as to have "expressed interest in purchasing homemade grenades," investigators wrote in the report.

Assistant Commonwealth's Attorney James Entas prosecuted the Robertson murder cases in state court. The threats of violence against gang witnesses, and Hayward specifically, were real, he said.

To strike at the Bloods, someone needed to step forward. Someone from the inside. Someone credible and strong.

Entas said Hayward was intelligent and personable from the start. But he said veteran investigators knew better than to trust any cooperating witness completely.

Soon after giving her statement, Hayward met with Coggeshall, detectives and prosecutors in the recreation room at Tidewater Detention Home, a juvenile facility in Chesapeake. They sat at work tables, surrounded by children's art projects hanging on the walls.

Hayward looked around at the men. They wore suits like mobsters, she thought. They wanted information: names, nicknames, faces, the culture.

"I just filled in the blanks," she said.

In other prisons, inmates in isolation, or protective custody, generally spend time outside their cells with other inmates every day. In Virginia, prisoners in protective custody go to meals and recreation as a group, a department of corrections spokesman said.

Hayward, under high security at the Norfolk jail, was more confined.

She left her cell just twice a week for trips to the jail gym and twice for showers. Medical and legal appointments afforded sporadic releases.

For days at a time, she stayed in her oddly shaped cell, roughly 8 feet by 15 feet at its widest points. High ceilings, white walls, a bed, a sink, a toilet and a television. The steel door had a cut-out of dense mesh with a rectangular chuck-hole for sliding through food trays.

Hayward was kept in the psychiatric wing, which housed female prisoners with mental illness or who needed high security. One inmate was accused of killing her child. The wing sometimes filled with shouts and wailing.

Some prisoners remain on high security status for a few weeks because media coverage is intense, said Maj. Angela Bennett, who supervised the jail's daily operations. Hayward remained there during her entire incarceration for her own safety, Bennett said.

During the first several months, she became depressed and withdrawn. She refused to eat. Jailers fed her cups of chipped ice to calm her nerves. They gave her prescription drugs to quell the anxiety.

She cut her hair to the scalp with a dry razor. She wrote lyrics: "Im so lonely its alarming/ I need people surround me/ Oh no shelter for whats coming/ It's my past and you must flee."

She slept so much she got bed sores, she said.

Yet sleep offered no escape. Nightmares raged. One recurred regularly: gang members finding her, and a man shooting her in the head.

Hundreds of homicide cases have been tried in the aging downtown Circuit Court since it opened in the late 1960s.

Few could match the breadth and scope of James Robertson's murder.

Police and federal agents arrested more than a dozen Bounty Hunter Blood gang members and associates in the months following his death. They leaned heavily on Hayward and, to a lesser extent, other gang members for evidence.

Coggeshall met Hayward in secure jail rooms. Entire floors were locked down when she left her cell to speak with him. They reviewed details of the beating again and again. He told her what to expect from each defense attorney. She was a quick study, he said.

The complicated cases moved slowly through the courts. Some ended up before federal judges.

The victim's parents came from Georgia for the hearings. Vera Robertson wrote to the court: "As I looked at the guys and girls in court telling their story about what happened, I wanted to holla out and asked them WHY? If they only knew how much he meant to everyone and how it have changed our lives drastically."

In all, 11 people were convicted of murder in Robertson's death. Police and prosecutors believe it's the most defendants ever convicted in the state for a single homicide. Hayward's co-defendants received between 11 years and life.

Two Big Homies were also locked away for life for other crimes.

After other witnesses set the scene for the jury, Hayward would take the stand. She wore a gray-and-black Norfolk jail jumper and chains. She was fueled by a pretrial snack of Hershey's bars, a Bible at her side.

She had a habit of looking people in the eye, listening to questions and answering them. She appeared calm, matter-of-fact and articulate most of the time. She acknowledged her role.

At one trial, Entas asked whether she could have told her story to police before they arrested her.

"No," Hayward testified. "I felt like my life would have been threatened, most definitely would have been killed. ... I mean, 'it's a love and loyalty' is what they say in the gang, the love and loyalty, and I didn't have that to them, to the gang, but I still didn't want to tell. I just didn't want anything to happen to myself nor my family."

She grew nervous before hearings for two Big Homies, Mikal Mix and Gary L. Toliver Jr. She rarely looked at any defendants, her former friends, until she was asked to identify them.

A federal prosecutor wrote to the court that Mix, a kingpin, was convicted on one count specifically on Hayward's testimony. "She clearly left an impression on the jury," Assistant U.S. Attorney William Muhr said. "Ms. Hayward was undoubtedly scared to death to testify ... but she told the jury that she was testifying because it was the right thing to do."

She fretted before the federal trial of Xavier Davis, a 16-year-old accused of stomping Robertson into the asphalt. Hayward and her family had taken in and fed Davis, a runaway. "Zae" was like a little brother, she said. Davis pleaded guilty before she had to testify.

Some of the city's most prominent defense attorneys blistered her on cross-examination and in closing arguments.

B. Thomas Reed, attorney for Nichelle Carter, said his client's conviction "never would have happened" without Hayward's testimony.

Reed argued to jurors that Hayward hid details about her role and that she had stoked male gang members into a frenzy.

In closing arguments, Reed asked jurors to see Hayward as the catalyst to the entire robbery and attack. "Skyler's testimony begs the question: How many lies does it take to make one a liar? Must I show you 10? Five? One?"

Entas asked jurors to trust a former gang member. "What \ as Skyler's demeanor?" he told jurors. "Yes, you might think it was arrogant and flip ... but she held her own against a very experienced and very talented defense attorney. She answered back."

Juries in several trials reached similar conclusions—Hayward's tight view of the gang, and her version about the attack, rang true.

Weeks and months after reaching verdicts, jurors contacted Entas and asked, "What's going to happen to Skyler?"

Coggeshall began to realize that part of advocating for his client was keeping her alert and healthy in solitary. Whenever he went to visit other clients, he stopped at Hayward's cell. Slowly, she began to open up.

He took her calls from jail after work. He put the telephone on speaker, played the keyboard and sang. Coggeshall favored upbeat '60s pop songs, from the Dave Clark Five and The Rascals. He was not Beyonce, but it made her laugh.

Hayward found another way out—books. Reading took her to a faraway place, she said.

She devoured the Twilight series, staying up three days straight. Next came tales of Anita Blake, a vampire hunter and U.S. marshal from St. Louis. Blake raises the dead and executes vampires.

Coggeshall spent more than $500 out of his own pocket sending her paperbacks from Barnes & Noble.

On her 21st birthday, after she had spent four years in solitary, lawyers arranged for a meeting at the police operations center. In reality, it was a birthday party. She wrote instructions to Coggeshall in a letter, with a smiley face and imperative at the top: "Do Not Deviate!!"

She wanted two large pizzas, hot wings, grape soda and a DVD player to show the first season of *True Blood*. She asked for balloons, in pink and purple, not red. She was old enough to drink and young enough to demand candles that spelled out "21."

In the four years when Granby classmates went to college or found jobs, Hayward studied and passed her high school equivalency exam. She spoke to at-risk children visiting on jail tours. She stared at that cell door, still not knowing when it would open.

Hayward was the last defendant sentenced.

Coggeshall researched the effects of solitary confinement on inmates before the final hearing. He discovered a United Nations report finding isolation could cause long-term psychological damage. Other experts have called for the practice to be banned.

The judge released Hayward in June with time served.

"It's a travesty that she ends up with the least time," said Emily Munn, a Norfolk defense attorney who represented Ieshia Rountree, who was convicted in the case in 2009.

Entas disagreed. Hayward's information and testimony proved accurate, he said. "Justice was served."

Entas mused in his office a few weeks ago: "Do I think we could have done it without her? I think it would have been a lot harder."

Police statistics show violent crime is down in Ocean View.

At his office, Coggeshall kept score in a folder.

Hayward testified against eight gang members. Each was convicted. She had a hand in more than a dozen cases, all told.

The lawyer says the five-year case was a good deal for the state to clean up gang-ridden neighborhoods. He recently submitted a bill for $31,000. It's the largest he's ever submitted and ever heard of. He hasn't received full payment.

Coggeshall also keeps a two-page letter Hayward wrote after four years in solitary.

"Dear Johnny The Kid," it begins. His client confesses that she never had a good male role model.

"Country girl in the big city chewed up and spit out. I had to get smart," Hayward wrote. "I know that you said you never had any kids but you make any kid proud to call you dad ...

"You've given so much and I have given you nothing. I feel like such a moocher. I value everything you buy me and your time and I don't say it enough. Thank you so much for everything. I never had this much in life given to me without a price tag. I know that's bad but it's true. But I want to thank you for being my angel in disguise."

Coggeshall still cries when he reads it.

Several weeks ago, Hayward met a reporter at a hotel room in another state. Coggeshall was at her side. They bantered like old friends.

The pair had declined interview requests over several months. They finally agreed to tell their story, as long as Hayward's safety was protected. They did not reveal any details about where Hayward and her family live and work.

Hayward started immediately with a question: What do you want to know? At 22, she had shared her life story with a great many strangers, and she's cautious. "I know I'm free," she said. "I'm still breaking off layer after layer."

The nightmares have passed, but safety is still a concern.

Virginia does not have a witness protection program. Authorities declined Hayward's request to be admitted into the federal system, Coggeshall said.

As a newly released convict, Hayward lacks money, medical care and a circle of dependable friends.

Some days, a bag of chips was her breakfast, lunch and dinner.

"I would love to pay a bill that's mine."

She has applied for dozens of jobs, she said. Once, she tried to explain her felony conviction to a potential employer. "Epic fail," Hayward said and laughed.

But she presses on. "Anything in this world worth having, you gotta fight for it."

Coggeshall interrupted, "It's like a 100-round prize fight. You got to come out swinging every round."

"Yeah! Every time," Hayward said. "Get up, and go for another round."

Hayward plans to go to community college, although she's not sure what she wants to study. She recently landed a full-time job and moved into a new place with her own room. Her worldly possessions fill three suitcases by her bed.

She has a view.

"I've got a little window I can open and close," she said. "Nice-sized window, actually."

Soldiers Recount 60-Second Attack That Left Them Reflecting on Life and Death

STARS AND STRIPES

MAY 1, 2012

By Martin Kuz

MUCHAI KALAY, Afghanistan —Staff Sgt. Damian Remijio and Spc. Zachary Fitch lay on the ground as a grenade bounced down a pile of rocks toward them. Metal struck stone with awful clarity.

Ting ... ting ... ting ...

Remijio spoke the words he believed would be his last.

"Tell Ashley I love her." His girlfriend of a year. "Tell Leiah I love her." His 3-year-old daughter.

"Tell them I'm sorry."

***

The soldiers belong to Company D of the 1st Battalion, 501st Infantry Regiment stationed at Combat Outpost Sabari in eastern Khost province.

Their platoon came under attack during a patrol April 12 near Muchai Kalay, a maze of mud-walled homes 15 miles from Pakistan.

Earlier that afternoon, a mortar round hit 100 feet outside COP Sabari, the fourth time in two weeks that militants had targeted the base. The artillery strikes suggested the so-called fighting season of the Taliban-led insurgency had arrived in a region dominated by the Haqqani network.

Command staff in the tactical operations center determined the mortar had been fired from the vicinity of Muchai Kalay. The U.S. platoon and one from the Afghan National Army drove three miles from the base to the village outskirts.

The soldiers climbed out of their armored trucks to search for the firing site in the dun-colored hills ringing the village. After 90 minutes, they had found nothing and headed back toward their vehicles parked beside a large wadi, or dry riverbed.

The wadi snakes through Muchai Kalay and several neighboring villages scattered across a wide valley whose scabbed, rock-strewn terrain is striped with lush farm fields nourished by the spring snowmelt. As the men walked, gunfire pelted down from high above, joined moments later by a sustained barrage from Muchai Kalay.

Bullets pocked the earth around them as they dived for cover. Gunners in the U.S. trucks sprayed the hills with fire from .50-caliber machine guns, buying time for the soldiers on the ground to start shooting. They took aim at the hidden attackers in the hills and what appeared to be two men in the village.

The firefight subsided after 20 minutes. Remijio, 26, of Chicago, coordinated a search for the gunmen in Muchai Kalay. The squad leader ordered three soldiers to circle around a cluster of buildings where the platoon had seen the assailants.

He and Fitch, 20, of Lenexa, Kansas, approached the buildings from the opposite side. They stopped outside a dirt alley that runs between the remnants of a pair of roofless stone homes.

Remijio peeked around the corner. He spotted two bearded faces, partially obscured by a wall about 60 feet away, near one end of the alley.

The passageway is the width of a sidewalk. Remijio walked roughly halfway to the end. He looked behind him as Fitch rounded the corner.

"Watch my back," Remijio said.

He turned forward again. The two bearded men had stepped into the alley and stood within 30 feet of him. They opened fire with AK-47s.

His armored vest absorbed two shots to the chest. The impact punched him to the ground. He curled up, gasping for breath.

Fitch squeezed the trigger on his M249 machine gun. The 5.56-millimeter rounds chewed up the walls, spitting out divots of rock. The AK-47s continued to chatter. Doorways offered thin cover as he moved from side to side down the alley.

Bullets whirred above Remijio in both directions until three shots hit Fitch. Two thudded against his vest. The third ripped through his left calf, blood blackening his green camouflage pants. He collapsed to the dirt an arm's length from the fallen sergeant.

Remijio rose to his feet, his lungs straining for air. He lifted his M4 automatic rifle and peered through the scope.

The alley opens to a field that slopes downward beyond the crumbling buildings. The two attackers had retreated to a doorway on his left about 30 feet away.

One at a time, the men ran from the doorway, trying to slip out of the alley and behind the abandoned home on Remijio's right.

He missed the first man with two shots. One of his next two rounds struck the second man in the back above the kidneys. His body jerked, a bright red bloom soaking through his white tunic.

The man staggered forward. Before vanishing from view, he snapped his left arm sideways in a throwing motion.

Remijio didn't see the grenade. His reaction relied on instinct and experience.

He dropped down to wrap his body around the injured Fitch to protect him from shrapnel. The grenade landed amid a mound of rocks a few feet in front of them and tumbled in their direction.

Ting … ting … ting …

"Tell Ashley I love her. Tell Leiah I love her. Tell them I'm sorry."

"What? Why?" Fitch asked.

He had heard the clinking of the grenade, but he was disoriented after being shot.

He struggled to pull free. Remijio hugged him tight. Their faces were almost touching.

***

Remijio opened his eyes. "Where am I?" he thought. "Am I dead? Alive?"

He turned his head. The dark alley walls framed a strip of pale blue sky.

Fitch needed no help from above. He knew from the throbbing in his calf that he had lived.

The smoke cleared. Remijio untangled himself from Fitch. Only then did they notice a low stone wall, 2 feet high and half as thick, jutting several inches into the alley. The wall, perhaps the vestige of a corridor between the homes, had stopped the grenade and shielded them from the blast.

At least one of the attackers lingered after the explosion. He fired three shots. Remijio felt a slight burning in his upper left arm. A bullet had bored into the front and out the back.

He assumed it was nothing more than a graze. He radioed for help before dressing Fitch's leg wound.

"Your shoulder," Fitch said.

"It's not that bad," Remijio said.

"No, man. You got shot."

Remijio looked closely at his wound for the first time. The sight of blood and shredded flesh beneath his torn shirt somehow sharpened the pain. He rolled off his knees and sat down.

Other members of the platoon arrived and began treating Fitch, whose injury was more severe.

An Afghan combat medic worked on Remijio's arm. Helicopters were en route to ferry the wounded men to Forward Operating Base Salerno, a 15-minute flight to the south.

The alley fight lasted 60 seconds at most, a span that cleaved each man's life in two. There is the time before walking into the alley, and all that happens after. In between is an everlasting minute.

***

Medics at FOB Salerno cleaned out Remijio's wound and swaddled his shoulder in padding. He lay in bed in the base hospital's intensive care unit waiting for Fitch to come out of surgery.

Remijio has soft, dark eyes and a lean frame hardened by weight lifting. A tattoo draping his right bicep that shows a pair of crosses testifies to his Catholic faith. A tattoo on his left arm of the Grim Reaper alludes to death's proximity in war.

Fitch, his boyish face topped with spiky black hair, talks at a pace that matches the rapid-fire bursts of the heavy machine gun he carries on patrol. His absence from the hospital room created a silence that cinched tight around Remijio.

The duo grew close in garrison in Anchorage, Alaska, where the 501st is stationed at Fort Richardson. Workout partners and video-game rivals, they share a bond rooted in the relentless banter of young men.

They deployed to Afghanistan with the 501st in December. Six years older than Fitch, who had never seen combat, Remijio served two tours in Iraq.

He felt accountable for the younger man's injury. It was a concern born not of guilt but of fraternal devotion. Fitch had risked his life to reach him in the alley.

Remijio dozed off. Sometime after midnight, he heard nurses help Fitch into the bed beside him.

"You OK?" Remijio asked.

"Yeah," Fitch replied with a drowsy smile, "I'm OK."

They fell into their familiar repartee, joking about the firefight, threatening to punch one another's wounds. The room's silence dissolved in laughter.

***

Remijio returned to COP Sabari four days later. The mental aftershocks from the ambush had yet to recede.

Moments from the alley swirled in his mind. The bullets cutting the air as he lay on the ground after being shot in the chest. The fear in the eyes of the two bearded men. The seconds before the grenade blew.

His heart rate accelerated when the images invaded. The dread crept into dreams, fracturing his sleep.

Four days after rejoining his unit, eight days after he was wounded, Remijio went on a patrol with his platoon. Heavy rain poured from low clouds as their trucks rolled out of the base.

Sweat saturated the T-shirt under his uniform. He took deep breaths and sipped water from a plastic bottle.

He told himself he would not allow memories of the alley to paralyze him.

The anxiety waned as he focused on the work at hand. The patrol proved to be uneventful, and four hours later, the platoon drove back to the outpost. Remijio gave unspoken thanks. He had reclaimed a small piece of something lost inside.

Panic attacks still plague him. Sleep remains elusive. But the shooting inspired an epiphany, changing his perspective on the war and the Army.

His trauma has given him greater sympathy for the suffering of Afghans and, in turn, deepened his pride in the U.S. military for attempting to aid them. Before his injury, he intended to leave the service after his contract ends in two years. He now leans toward re-enlisting.

"You want to make a difference," he said.

Fitch came back to COP Sabari last week. In the platoon's barracks, he ran into Remijio, who approached with his arms spread wide.

"Hug it out," Remijio said as they embraced.

"Hey, man," Fitch replied, "good to see you."

Fitch had no desire to re-enlist before he was shot. He has not reconsidered.

Like Remijio, he struggles with thoughts that flood in unbidden. Watching his friend fall to the ground and believing he might be dead. The pain that surged through him after the bullet pierced his leg. The blackness as the grenade detonated.

He thinks of the stone wall that absorbed the blast, appearing as the smoke dissipated as if willed into reality. "It's why we're alive," Fitch said.

He is 20 years old. Death is no longer abstract.

Judges' Profiles

Figure 1. Top to bottom: Roger Thurow, Maria Carrillo, and Michele Weldon

Roger Thurow spent two decades as *The Wall Street Journal*'s foreign correspondent, based in Europe and Africa. His coverage of global affairs spanned the Cold War, the release of Nelson Mandela, the end of apartheid, the wars in the former Yugoslavia and the humanitarian crises of the first decade of this century—along with 10 Olympic Games. In 2003, he and *Journal* colleague Scott Kilman wrote a series of stories on famine in Africa that was a finalist for the Pulitzer Prize in International Reporting. Their reporting on humanitarian and development issues was also honored by the United Nations. Thurow and Kilman are authors of the book, *Enough: Why the World's Poorest Starve in an Age of Plenty*. In 2009, they were awarded Action Against Hunger's Humanitarian Award. They also received the 2009 Harry Chapin Why Hunger book award. In May 2012, Thurow published his second book, *The Last Hunger Season: A Year in an African Farm Community on the Brink of Change*. In January 2010, Thurow joined The Chicago Council on Global Affairs as senior fellow for global agriculture and food policy.

Maria Carrillo is managing editor at *The Virginian-Pilot* in Norfolk, Virginia, where she remains committed to craft even in a Twitter world.

Her exceptional writers have been nationally recognized, including being Pulitzer and ASNE finalists. Carrillo has worked at *The Pilot* for 16 years, directing many of the paper's projects and previously overseeing its narrative team. That work has spawned five books so far, with a sixth on the way. Carrillo has been a visiting faculty member for The Poynter Institute and the Nieman program, a lecturer for the National Writers Workshops and the American Press Institute, and a Pulitzer juror four times.

Michele Weldon, a journalist and author, is assistant professor emerita in service in journalism at The Medill School, Northwestern University, where she has taught since 1996. She is director of Medill Public Thought Leaders and the Northwestern Public Voices Fellowship for The OpEd Project. She was co-director of TEDxNorthwesternU 2014. Her nonfiction books include *I Closed My Eyes, Writing to Save Your Life,* and *Everyman News: The Changing American Front Page*, which won the

National Federation of Press Women nonfiction book award in 2009. She has written columns, news and features for many newspapers, websites, magazines and radio. She has produced lessons for TED Ed and competed in the Moth Story Chicago GrandSlam. A popular public speaker, Weldon has delivered close to 200 keynotes across the country and Canada on issues related to women and the media, and has been a guest on hundreds of radio and television shows in the United States, Europe and Canada including *The Oprah Winfrey Show*, NBC's *Later Today*, *ABC Sunday Morning*, and BBC-TV. She is a board member of Global Girl Media, a former member of the board of directors of Journalism and Women Symposium and has been a seminar leader with The OpEd Project since 2011.

Figure 2. Roy Peter Clark (left) and Mike Wilson (right)

Roy Peter Clark has taught writing at the Poynter Institute, a school for journalists in St. Petersburg, Florida, since 1979. He has served Poynter as dean, senior scholar, and vice president and is often described as the most influential writing coach in American journalism. He is the author or editor of 16 books, the most recent of which are *Writing Tools, The Glamour of Grammar,* and *Help! For Writers*. He is often quoted in news stories about language, politics, sports and American culture. His work has been featured on NPR, CNN and the Oprah Winfrey Show. He thinks of himself as a garage band legend, often using music in his writing workshops. *The New York Times* described his book *The Glamour of Grammar* as "very much a manual for the 21st century."

Mike Wilson is the former managing editor of the *Tampa Bay Times*, responsible for the day-to-day operation of the newspaper and Tampabay.com. Wilson came to the *Times* in 1995 after 12 years as a writer and editor at the *Miami Herald*. In his career at the *Times*, he has worked as a reporter, features editor, assistant managing editor for features and managing editor for enterprise. In 2009, a member of his feature writing staff, Lane DeGregory, won the Pulitzer Prize for feature writing for "The Girl in the Window." A second journalist on his staff, John Barry, was a finalist that year for the Pulitzer in features. Before becoming an editor, Wilson won national and regional awards for feature writing, and in 1998 was part of a team whose reporting on a corrupt Baptist minister was a finalist for the Pulitzer for investigative reporting. Wilson is on the boards of the Florida Society of News Editors and *Florida Trend* magazine and has served as a juror for the Pulitzer Prizes. He has written two books, *Right on the Edge of Crazy* (1993), about the U.S. downhill ski team, and *The Difference Between God and Larry Ellison* (1997), about the chief executive of Oracle Corp. A native of Connecticut, he graduated from Tufts University in Medford, Mass.

CPSIA information can be obtained at www.ICGtesting.com
Printed in the USA
LVOW06s1158190614

390794LV00004B/7/P